SCHOLASTIC

YEAR IN SPORTS
2015

SCHOLASTIC INC.

Copyright © 2015 by Shoreline Publishing Group LLC

All rights reserved. Published by Scholastic Inc., *Publishers since 1920*.
SCHOLASTIC and associated logos are trademarks and/or registered trademarks of Scholastic Inc.

ISBN 978-0-545-67953-4

10 9 8 7 6 5 4 3 2 1   14 15 16 17

Printed in the U.S.A.   40
First edition, December 2014

Produced by Shoreline Publishing Group LLC

Due to the publication date, records, results, and statistics are current as of August 2014.

CONTENTS

Sports World!

You might have heard the expression "the world of sports," right? Well, in 2013 and 2014, that was more true than ever! Over and over in that time span, the eyes of the world turned together to the world of sports. We spend most of our time rooting for our favorite teams, and mostly in sports played in North America. But in 2014, two of the biggest worldwide sporting events took place and billions of people tuned in, eager to share in the joy of victory. Or maybe just to get some time off from school or work to cheer!

The first big international event was the 2014 Winter Olympics in Sochi, Russia. Though some winter sports don't get much attention in non-Olympic years, none of that mattered when the skaters, skiers, bobsledders, and snowboarders got into action going for gold. New heroes were crowned, new records set, and more Olympic memories were created. What was your favorite? Check out our report on the Games starting on page 54.

After the snow had melted and the Olympic winter athletes were headed back to wherever they wait until the next Winter Games (mark your calendars now: South Korea, 2018!), it was time for the world to pay attention to the world's most popular sport: soccer, or, as most of the world calls it, football.

Flags of nations paraded at the Olympic closing ceremonies.

Fans flocked to Brazil to watch the World Cup. Those who could not be there in person watched in their homes, in restaurants, or at huge outdoor rallies in big cities. No matter what you call it, the sport connects more people than any other. People are intense fans of their home countries' teams, but once their country is out, they still tune in to watch the planet's best players.

And those players put on an amazing show of great goals, masterful goalkeeping, and ankle-twisting dribbling. In the end, only one country's fans were truly happy, but everyone else had a great time, too. We have all the action starting on page 64.

Basketball rivals soccer for popularity around the world. Just before he left for a summer trip to China, **LeBron James** gained world attention by announcing that he was moving from the Miami Heat back

Germany's Phillip Lahm with the World Cup!

"home" to the Cleveland Cavaliers. "The King" and his new court will try to become hometown heroes . . . and world champs.

The NFL crowned a new champion as the Seattle Seahawks won their first Super Bowl. More and more international fans are tuning in to the NFL, so look for Seahawks jerseys to pop up in international cities soon!

From the Olympics to the World Cup, the world of sports continues to get bigger and bigger . . . and to come closer and closer together thanks to TV and social media. But there's still nothing like a book to pull it all together.

So sit back, read on, and look back on the wonderful, wide, and sometimes wacky world of sports.

MOMENTS IN SPORTS
SEPTEMBER 2013 ▶ AUGUST 2014

Time for our annual countdown! No, we're not sending a rocket to space (though that would be cool, right?). Instead, we're looking back over a year of amazing sports events and choosing the top 10 most memorable, most amazing, most earth-shattering, and just plain most awesome! From stunning come-from-behind victories to history-making losses . . . from the water to the turf to the ice . . . with pucks, balls, skates, gloves, sails, helmets, and words (words? Read on to find out how they made this list!)—the moments on the pages that follow have become a part of history.

The best thing about sports is that we know that as great as these moments were, there are even more amazing events coming in the months ahead. Will we see a play to top Auburn-Alabama? Will we see a bigger comeback than the America's Cup? Will a pitcher ever throw a better game than Clayton Kershaw?

Join us again in this space next year to find the answers to those questions. In the meantime, let's start the countdown . . . 10, 9, 8, 7 . . .

10 ANOTHER KIND OF CROWN The Los Angeles Kings won their second Stanley Cup in three seasons in 2014. This time around, though, they made their fans sweat (even though they were in icy arenas!). The Kings had to play seven games in each of the first three rounds of the playoffs. They became the first team to win three Game 7s on the road in one postseason.

9 **HANDS UP FOR SEATTLE** *This amazing fingertip block by Seattle's Richard Sherman of a last-minute 49ers pass was the play of the NFL season. The break-up sealed the NFC title for the Seahawks. In the ensuing Super Bowl, they romped over the Denver Broncos, shutting down the record-setting passing of Peyton Manning. It was the Seahawks' first Super Bowl championship.*

8 **SANDY WHO?** When you think of great Dodgers lefthanded pitchers, the legendary *Sandy Koufax* comes right to mind. After all, he threw four no-hitters, including a perfect game. But even that might not have been as good as LA's *Clayton Kershaw*. On June 19, 2014, he threw a no-hitter against the Rockies. Kershaw struck out 15, the most ever for a pitcher who also did not allow a single walk in the game. The only baserunner squeaked across on an infield error. Some stat experts ranked it one of the best two or three games ever pitched!

7

WHAT AN ENDING!! *The Auburn-Alabama game is always a huge matchup; some people call it the fiercest rivalry in college sports. The 2013 edition will go down in history. With the score tied and just a few seconds left, Alabama tried a 57-yard field goal. It was a decision Crimson Tide fans will be mad about for years. The kick was way short, and Auburn's Chris Davis caught it near the back of the end zone. A few seconds and 109 yards later, he had scored . . . untouched. Auburn won on what experts now call one of the greatest (if not THE greatest) ending to a college game ever.*

6

BOSTON STRONG! Before the 2014 season, most experts picked the Red Sox to finish at or near the bottom of the A.L. East, even with new manager *John Farrell* (pictured). In April, however, the team got a jolt of inspiration after a bomb hit the Boston Marathon. As the city rallied around the runners who were hurt, the Sox began to win . . . and win and win. They boasted the league's top offense, and their success raised the hopes of New England. In the end, they knocked off the Cardinals to win their third World Series crown of the 2000s.

5 **GOLDEN CANADA!** For the second Winter Olympics in a row, Canada (including forward *Jonathan Toews*, above) captured the gold medals the nation most wanted: in ice hockey. The Canadian men and women each brought home the Olympic championship. Along the way, both teams knocked off the American squads, making the gold doubly delicious!

4 ULTIMATE COMEBACK

Even if you do not follow yacht racing, you have to be impressed by what Team USA did in the 2013 America's Cup. To capture the Cup, one of the two finalists had to win nine head-to-head matches. Team New Zealand won eight of the first nine, opening up a commanding 8–1 margin. But somehow, Team USA clawed back. As the Kiwis got more and more desperate, the US kept charging to victory. Finally, tied 8–8, the two battled in a winner-take-all race . . . and Team USA did it again, capping one of sports' biggest comebacks.

3

THE AMAZING TIM HOWARD The American goalkeeper for the World Cup will probably not look back on this game fondly, since his team ended up losing to Belgium, 2–1. But to most American fans, the performance of *Tim Howard* was one of the highlights of the Cup, if not the whole year. He set an all-time World Cup record with 16 saves, including many diving, lunging stops. His offense could not back him up, however, and two late goals gave the Belgians the victory. But to Howard goes the title of "Gallant in Defeat."

2

WELCOME HOME! *Normally,* LeBron James *is the subject of sportswriters' praise. They've written about The King's two NBA titles and his MVP trophies and his big move to Miami. But in 2014, James became the writer. His article in* Sports Illustrated *announced to the world (and a very happy Ohio) that he was signing back up with the Cleveland Cavaliers. James grew up near Cleveland and played there from 2003–2010 (he is shown here from 2009). His homecoming (along with some other moves by the Cavs) make them a team to beat in 2015.*

1

THE OTHER FOOTBALL RULES! As more than a billion people in probably every country on Earth tuned in, the World Cup final was played in Rio de Janiero, Brazil. The world's most popular sporting event featured the South American flair of Argentina and Lionel Messi against the striking power and all-around skill of Germany. The Argentines bottled up the German attack for nearly 120 minutes. But this extra-time goal by *Mario Götze* gave Germany its fourth World Cup championship.

PLAY OF THE YEAR

Seattle's Richard Sherman sent the Seahawks to Super Bowl XLVIII with this last-second play in the NFC Championship Game. He knocked the ball to a teammate and kept San Francisco's Michael Crabtree from making the TD catch in the NFC Championship Game.

NFL: Eyes West!

If you were looking for the best teams in the NFL for the 2013 season, you had to head west. Five of the 12 playoff teams were from the two West divisions. A sixth team, the Arizona Cardinals from the NFC West, had 10 wins but didn't even make the postseason! Three of the four teams in the conference championship games were among West teams. And of course in the end, the farthest-west NFL team—the

Tom Brady and the Patriots nearly made the Super Bowl.

Seattle Seahawks—took home the Vince Lombardi Trophy as Super Bowl champs. (See the full story of that game on page 26.)

The AFC West's Kansas City Chiefs (okay, they're more Midwest, but that's their division!) got off to a hot start. New coach **Andy Reid** turned the team around; in 2012, the Chiefs had won only two games all season! In 2013, they won their first nine games. But their division rivals, the Denver Broncos, were even hotter. They won 11 of their first 13, including victories over the Chiefs twice in three weeks.

In the NFC West, the San Francisco 49ers continued a hot rivalry with the Seahawks. The Niners were defending NFC champs, but Seattle put them in their place with a big Week 2 win. After San Francisco lost to Indianapolis the next week, they rallied and quickly got back in the Super Bowl hunt. Coach **Jim Harbaugh** became the first coach to take his team to the conference championship game in each of his first three seasons.

Seattle was rolling, too, thanks to its 12th Man. The team's super-loud fans (see page 34) energized their team, which won all of its home games until a Week 16 loss to Arizona.

Let's not forget the East, though. The Carolina Panthers (okay, they play in the NFC South, but they're on the East Coast!) started 1–3. Then an eight-game winning streak, powered by multi-talented QB **Cam Newton**, put them back in the playoff chase. They ended

606

The number of points scored by the Denver Broncos in the regular season, an all-time NFL record.

The New England Patriots continued their decade-long run of success. However, in 2013, star QB **Tom Brady** had to work overtime. The team was hit by many injuries and he had to connect with new receivers. In fact, 14 different players caught passes for the Pats in 2013. But they found a way to win, and were the only non-West team in the conference championships.

As the playoffs began, all eyes were on the West. Fans and experts alike wanted to see one matchup in the Super Bowl: the record-setting offense of the Broncos against the rock-hard defense of the Seahawks. Everyone (except Denver) saw their wish come true.

up with the second-best record in the NFC.

Indianapolis Colts QB **Andrew Luck** continued to impress, guiding his team to 11 wins and a division title. Since taking over for **Peyton Manning**, Luck has become one of the game's best young leaders.

2013 Final Regular-Season Standings

AFC EAST	W	L	T
New England Patriots	12	4	
New York Jets	8	8	
Miami Dolphins	8	8	
Buffalo Bills	6	10	

AFC NORTH	W	L	T
Cincinnati Bengals	11	5	
Pittsburgh Steelers	8	8	
Baltimore Ravens	8	8	
Cleveland Browns	4	12	

AFC SOUTH	W	L	T
Indianapolis Colts	11	5	
Tennessee Titans	7	9	
Jacksonville Jaguars	4	12	
Houston Texans	2	14	

AFC WEST	W	L	T
Denver Broncos	13	3	
Kansas City Chiefs	11	5	
San Diego Chargers	9	7	
Oakland Raiders	4	12	

NFC EAST	W	L	T
Philadelphia Eagles	10	6	
Dallas Cowboys	8	8	
New York Giants	7	9	
Washington Redskins	3	13	

NFC NORTH	W	L	T
Green Bay Packers	8	7	1
Chicago Bears	8	8	
Detroit Lions	7	9	
Minnesota Vikings	5	10	1

NFC SOUTH	W	L	T
Carolina Panthers	12	4	
New Orleans Saints	11	5	
Atlanta Falcons	4	12	
Tampa Bay Buccaneers	4	12	

NFC WEST	W	L	T
Seattle Seahawks	13	3	
San Francisco 49ers	12	4	
Arizona Cardinals	10	6	
St. Louis Rams	7	9	

2013 Playoffs

Wild-Card Playoffs

Colts 45, Chiefs 44

Down by 28 points in the second half, **Andrew Luck** and the Colts put on the second-biggest rally in playoff history. Luck threw four TD passes and scored on a fumble recovery to lead the Colts. The two teams set a playoff record with 1,049 combined yards on offense.

Chargers 27, Bengals 10

A dream season for young quarterback **Andy Dalton** ended after the Bengals disappeared in a storm of turnovers. Dalton threw two picks and fumbled once. It was Cincinnati's first loss at home all year.

49ers 23, Packers 20

The cold was the big story in Green Bay: 5 degrees at kickoff, but San Francisco kicker **Phil Dawson** hit a 33-yard field goal on the game's final play to win the game.

Saints 26, Eagles 24

This was another nail-biter. New Orleans had to rally on the road to set up a chance at the game-winner. Saints kicker **Shayne Graham** had only been with the Saints for two weeks, but he came through with a final-play field goal to win.

Divisional Playoffs

Patriots 43, Colts 22

The Colts ran out of Andrew's "luck." The young QB threw four interceptions. **LaGarrette Blount** ran for four Patriots touchdowns as steady rain made the passing game difficult.

Luck (right) led the Comeback Colts in a playoff win.

Broncos 24, Chargers 17

In 2012, the Broncos tripped up in the divisional round. **Peyton Manning** made sure that didn't happen again. He threw two touchdowns and led the team to a game-clinching score by **Knowshon Moreno**.

49ers 23, Panthers 10

The Niners' defense was the star of this show. They sacked talented Panthers QB **Cam Newton** five times and picked him off twice. QB **Colin Kaepernick** was solid for San Francisco, who earned their third straight trip to the NFC title game.

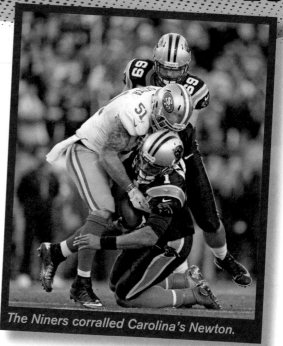

The Niners corralled Carolina's Newton.

Seahawks 23, Saints 15

Rain and wind made it perfect Seattle weather. Kicker **Steven Hauschka** battled the elements to make three field goals. **Marshawn Lynch** scored twice. And the mighty Seattle D did the rest, shutting down top passer **Drew Brees** and **Jimmy Graham**, whose 16 TD catches had led the NFL.

Conference Championships

Broncos 26, Patriots 16

This was the 15th time that **Peyton Manning** and New England's **Tom Brady** met in a game. Manning came out on top this time, throwing for 400 yards and directing an offense that controlled the clock to keep Brady off the field. Denver's **Matt Prater** had four field goals to keep the pressure on New England, who just could not get its offense rolling. Manning led another AFC team to the Super Bowl.

Seahawks 23, 49ers 17

Everyone was talking about the play by **Richard Sherman** to deny the Niners a touchdown on the final play (see page 20). But Seattle fans loved **Russell Wilson**'s clutch 4th-down, 35-yard TD strike to **Jermaine Kearse** for the go-ahead score. The Seattle defense bent but did not break under the attack of **Kaepernick**, who ran for a game-high 130 yards. Seattle would try to win its first Super Bowl against Manning and the Broncos.

Super Seahawks!

SUPER BOWL XLVIII · NEW YORK

Did the game end on Denver's first snap from center? Or did it end with Seattle's first interception of a **Peyton Manning** pass? Did it end with the second-quarter interception return that made it 22–0? Or was it **Percy Harvin's** shocking second-half kickoff return for a score?

Seattle's players all said that it had actually ended a week or so earlier. That's when the Seahawks, after studying the mighty Denver offensive machine, figured out how to shut it down. With that confidence, everything just went Seattle's way. They captured their first Super Bowl championship with a 43–8 win over the Broncos. It was the biggest victory margin in a Super Bowl since the 1992 season.

Denver had set records for most points in a season, while Manning had set regular-season passing records galore. Seattle's hard-nosed defense didn't care. They never let the Broncos get going. It didn't help that the first snap to Manning sailed over his head and ended up as a safety for Seattle.

At 12 seconds, it was the fastest score in Super Bowl history. The Seahawks got the ball back and then drove for a field goal. After holding Manning again, they drove for another field goal. Then they turned a Manning interception into a touchdown. In the first quarter, Denver gave up a safety and an interception and didn't have a single first down.

The tone of the game was set: Seattle would dominate throughout. In the second quarter, the Broncos finally got a drive going. Then a furious pass rush forced a poor throw by Manning. Seattle's **Malcolm Smith** returned the interception 69 yards for a score.

After a long halftime (nice show by **Bruno Mars**!), Percy Harvin put the game away. The speedy wide receiver had missed

Seattle's defense overpowered Moreno and the Broncos.

most of the season with a hip injury. Then he missed most of the playoffs with a concussion. He made up for lost time by returning the second-half kickoff 87 yards for a touchdown. It was 29–0 Seattle.

"We saw this coming," said defensive end **Michael Bennett**. "We never went into a game thinking we couldn't win. We always knew when we played our type of defense that we play, there's no offense that can play with us."

Wilson is a Super Bowl winner!

The Seahawks added two more TDs in the second half on touchdown passes by **Russell Wilson**. The Broncos prevented a shutout with a TD to end the third quarter, but it was far from enough.

The Seahawks put on one of the most dominating shows in recent Super Bowl history. Smith earned the game's MVP for his big pick, a fumble recovery, and nine tackles. But the entire Seattle D could have earned it together. Does great defense stop great offense? On Super Bowl Sunday, the answer was yes.

SUPER CITY!

The Super Bowl was held in the New York City area for the first time. Many worried that cold or snowy weather would bother fans and players. It was cold, but the snowstorm didn't happen. The game was played at MetLife Stadium, which is actually in New Jersey. New York City's famous street, Broadway, turned into Super Bowl Boulevard. Fans enjoyed block after block of NFL-themed fun, from a huge slide, to real goalposts, to booths for shopping. The big game did just fine in the Big Apple!

SUPER BOWL XLVIII

TEAM	1Q	2Q	3Q	4Q	FINAL
SEATTLE	8	14	14	7	43
DENVER	0	0	8	0	8

SCORING

1Q: SEA   C. Avril tackles K. Moreno in end zone

1Q: SEA   S. Hauschka, 31-yard FG

1Q: SEA   S. Hauschka, 33-yard FG

2Q: SEA   M. Lynch, 1-yard run (Haushcka kick)

2Q: SEA   M. Smith, 69-yard interception return (Haushka kick)

3Q: SEA   P. Harvin, 87-yard kickoff return (Hauschka kick)

3Q: SEA   J. Kearse, 23-yard pass from R. Wilson (Hauschka kick)

3Q: DEN   D. Thomas, 14-yard pass from P. Manning (Manning to Welker for 2-point)

4Q: SEA   D. Baldwin, 10-yard pass from R. Wilson (Hauschka kick)

Stat Champs

1,607 RUSHING YARDS
LeSean McCoy, Eagles

12 RUSHING TDS
Jamaal Charles, Chiefs
Marshawn Lynch, Seahawks

55 PASSING TDS

5,477 PASSING YARDS
Peyton Manning, Broncos

1,646 RECEIVING YARDS
Josh Gordon, Browns

113 RECEPTIONS
Pierre Garcon, Redskins

16 RECEIVING TDS
Jimmy Graham, Saints

158 POINTS
Stephen Gostkowski, Patriots

38 FIELD GOALS
Stephen Gostkowski, Patriots
Justin Tucker, Ravens

171 TACKLES
Vontaze Burfict, Bengals

19.5 SACKS
Robert Mathis, Colts

8 INTERCEPTIONS
Richard Sherman, Seahawks

Not even snow could stop McCoy's running.

AWARD WINNERS

NFL MVP

PEYTON MANNING
BRONCOS

OFFENSIVE PLAYER OF THE YEAR

PEYTON MANNING
BRONCOS

DEFENSIVE PLAYER OF THE YEAR

LUKE KUECHLY
PANTHERS

OFFENSIVE ROOKIE OF THE YEAR

EDDIE LACY
PACKERS

DEFENSIVE ROOKIE OF THE YEAR

SHELDON RICHARDSON
JETS

COMEBACK PLAYER OF THE YEAR

PHILIP RIVERS
CHARGERS

COACH OF THE YEAR

RON RIVERA
PANTHERS

WALTER PAYTON AWARD
(Given for community service)

CHARLES TILLMAN
BEARS

Magic Manning

Three seasons ago, many thought **Peyton Manning** was done. But he battled back from a neck injury, moved from the Colts to the Broncos, and turned another team into an AFC contender. Even though his team lost the Super Bowl, it was a complete non-surprise that Manning was named the MVP for the fifth time, more than any player in the 94-year history of the NFL. (Bonus Fact! **Jim Brown**, **Brett Favre**, and **Johnny Unitas** each were MVP three times.)

Mr.64

The NFL record for longest field goal stood since 1971 at 63 yards. Three players matched that mark but none had gone past it…until **Matt Prater** lined up for a 64-yard attempt on December 8 in Denver. The Broncos kicker nailed the kick and set a new standard for long-distance kicking!

1st Quarter

NFL WEEKS 1-4

✳ Super Seven: In Week 1, Denver's **Peyton Manning** tied an NFL record by throwing seven touchdown passes. The Broncos smacked the defending-champion Ravens 49–27.

✳ Close Calls: Twelve of the 16 games in Week 1 were decided by seven or fewer points. That's tied for the most ever on a weekend in NFL history! And eight teams came back in the fourth quarter to win.

> **"Peyton is phenomenal. To continue to come out every year and put that kind of performance on for us, it's amazing."**
>
> — DENVER TIGHT END **JULIUS THOMAS**

✳ Time Out for Mother Nature: Lightning interrupted the big Sunday night showdown between San Francisco and Seattle. When the storm passed, the Seahawks just kept raining down on **Colin Kaepernick**. Seattle won easily, 29–3.

✳ Talented Twosome: In Green Bay's 38–20 defeat of Washington, the Packers were the first team ever to have a passer with 450-plus yards (**Aaron Rodgers** with a team-record 480) and a runner with 125-plus yards (**James Starks**'s 132).

✳ Unwelcome Home: In Week 3, Coach **Andy Reid** returned to Philly and stomped his old team, 26–16. His new team, the Chiefs, had already passed their 2012 victory total of two wins.

✳ Soaring Scores: Carolina kept the Giants winless with a 38–0 pounding, as **Cam Newton** threw for three TDs. Seattle also had a scoring binge, putting up 45 points to beat Jacksonville.

✳ Fabulous Four: **Manning** kept rolling, as Denver scored a team-record 52 points while beating Philadelphia. Manning's 16 TD passes in the first four games set a new record.

Rodgers and Starks teamed to set records.

2nd Quarter

NFL WEEKS 5-8

✳ Shootout in Dallas: In Week 5, **Peyton Manning** and **Tony Romo** lit up the enormous scoreboard at Cowboys Stadium. Denver won the shootout 51–48 on a last-play field goal by **Matt Prater**. The 99 points was the fourth-highest total in an NFL game.

✳ Ouch: After struggling in early games, the 49ers showed the promise of their 2012 NFC championship, rocking the Texans, 34–3, in Week 5. In the game, Houston QB **Matt Schaub** set an unfortunate record by giving up a pick-six in his fourth straight game.

Stafford's surprise score made winners of the Lions over Dallas.

✳ Comeback King: Though nearly all of his starting receivers were injured, **Tom Brady** of the Patriots still pulled a rabbit out of the hat in Week 6. He led the Patriots to a game-winning drive over the Saints, throwing the game-winning TD pass with five seconds left.

✳ Happy Returns: Chicago's **Devin Hester** carried a punt to the end zone. It was his 20th return score, and he passed **Deion Sanders** for most of all time. But Washington's **Roy Helu** had three TD runs and the Redskins won in Week 7.

✳ Lucky 7?: Six of this week's games ended on very late scores, including four on final-play field goals!

✳ Sneaky Win: Detroit QB **Matthew Stafford** had a trick up his sleeve. After leading the Lions' to the Dallas one-yard line with just a few seconds left, he dove over the line to score. Everyone was expecting him to spike the ball and stop the clock, but he decided just to win the game! **Calvin "Megatron" Johnson** was the other big story in this game. His 329 receiving yards were the second-most ever in an NFL game.

✳ Hello, London!: Maybe the Jaguars were jet-lagged. They got whomped by the 49ers, 42–10, in London's Wembley Stadium.

3rd Quarter
NFL WEEKS 9-12

✳ A Timely Two: Here's something you don't see every week. The Dolphins sacked Cincinnati's **Andy Dalton** in the end zone in Week 9. What made it unusual? The safety came in overtime, giving Miami the win on a walkoff safety!

✳ Nick's Sixes: In Week 7, for only the seventh time ever, but the second time in 2013, an NFL QB threw 7 TDs in a game. Philadelphia's **Nick Foles** matched **Peyton Manning**'s as Week 1 feat.

✳ Patriot Pounding: **Tom Brady** led New England to a 55-31 win over Pittsburgh. The Patriots became only the third team since 1970 with 600 or more yards and 50-plus points. The game also saw the most points ever given up by the Steelers.

✳ Austin's Power: In Week 10, Rams fans enjoyed The **Tavon Austin** Show. In a win over the Colts, the rookie had three scores of 50-plus yards—a 98-yard punt return and TD catches of 57 and 81 yards.

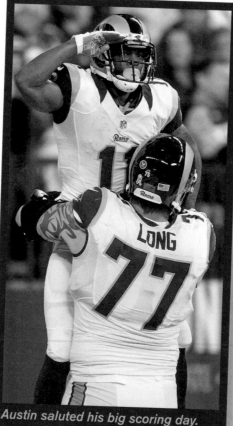

Austin saluted his big scoring day.

✳ Lose the Zeroes: Finally, in Week 10, the Jaguars and Buccaneers each won their first game of the year, beating Tennessee and Miami. Then in Week 11, the Chiefs finally lost a game. After starting 9-0, they became the last NFL team to lose. The Broncos and **Peyton Manning** beat them 27-17 on Sunday night.

✳ Double Comeback: In Week 12, the Patriots rallied from 24 points down to beat Denver in overtime. After a trio of fumbles in the first half, New England was down 24-0 at halftime but the Pats scored 31 consecutive points to take the lead. Then Denver made its own comeback, tying the game. In overtime, a punt muff by the Broncos set up the Pats' game-winning field goal.

✳ Even-Steven: The NFL had a time game for the second straight year when the Vikings and Packers each scored 26 points in Week 12. Both teams made a field goal in overtime, but under the new rules, it was not sudden death. When the 15 minutes ended without a touchdown, the game was over.

4th Quarter
NFL WEEKS 13–17

∗ Gordo!: Cleveland receiver **Josh Gordon** became the first NFL player ever with back-to-back 200-yard receiving games. The Browns lost the game in which he set it, however, falling to Jacksonville, 32–28, in Week 13.

∗ Hey, Coach…Move!: Baltimore stopped Pittsburgh's attempt to tie their game with a late two-point conversion and won 22–20 in Week 13. Earlier in the game, Steelers coach **Mike Tomlin** stepped slightly onto the field in the path of Baltimore kick returner **Jacoby Jones**. Jones was tackled and didn't score; Tomlin was later fined by the NFL for being on the field illegally.

∗ Late Magic: New England's **Tom Brady** had two touchdown passes in the final 61 seconds to spark a big comeback over Cleveland in Week 14.

∗ The Candlestick Goes Out: In the next-to-last game at San Francisco's Candlestick Park, the hometown 49ers won a big NFC West showdown with the Seahawks. **Phil Dawson** nailed a 22-yard kick near the end for the 19–17 win.

∗ Lights Out: Scoreboards around the NFL got a workout in Week 14. Some of the high-scoring results: 51 for Broncos, 45 for the Chiefs and Bears, 42 for the Bengals, and two 37s.

∗ Charles in Charge: Kansas City running back **Jamaal Charles** put on a show in Week 15. He scored five touchdowns as the Chiefs got into playoff shape with a 56–31 win over the Raiders.

∗ Kick Six: Baltimore's **Justin Tucker** nailed a 61-yard field goal in the final minute to give the Ravens the win over the Lions. It was Tucker's sixth FG of the game!

∗ Oops: In Week 16, all the Lions had to do to clinch a playoff spot was beat the Giants, who had lost 9 games entering the contest. But Detroit lost 23–20 in overtime.

∗ The Pack! The playoffs started early. In Week 17, the Packers and Bears met in an NFC North showdown. The winner would get a playoff berth. The Packers welcomed back injured QB **Aaron Rodgers**, who threw a game-winning pass to **Randall Cobb** to clinch the division title.

Jamaal Charles

NFL News and Notes

As always, a ton of NFL records fell during the season. Here's a look at some of the most amazing stats.

11,985

The entire league combined to set a new all-time scoring record with 11,985 points. The per-game average of 46.8 was the highest ever! Eleven NFL teams scored at least 400 points, also a new record.

Double-Digits

For the first time ever, a team had five players score 10 or more touchdowns in a season. That team was (no surprise) the Denver Broncos. The players were **Demaryius Thomas**, **Knowshon Moreno**, **Julius Thomas**, **Eric Decker**, and **Wes Welker**.

137.6

The Seattle Seahawks not only won a Super Bowl, their fans got a world record. During the team's December 2 game against New Orleans, Seattle's fans set a new noise mark. Their cheers reached 137.6 decibels . . . a jet taking off is only about 140 decibels!

On a team full of touchdown catchers, Demaryius Thomas led the way with 14.

NFL Fantasy Stars

Did you have these guys on your fantasy team? If you did, you were pretty lucky . . . and pretty good. Fantasy football connects millions of people every week. If you're not playing, you should give it a try and see if you can put together a winning team. Here are the top fantasy point scorers per position in 2013, according to NFL.com.

QB: **Peyton Manning**, 410.0 points

RB: **Jamaal Charles**, 308.0

WR: **Josh Gordon**, 227.4 ▶▶▶

TE: **Jimmy Graham**, 217.5

K: **Stephen Gostkowski**, 168.0

D/ST: **Chiefs**, 204.0

Pass-Happy

Quarterbacks combined for 24 games with 400 or more yards passing. The previous record was only 18!

Good Start

Seattle's **Russell Wilson** led his team to 24 wins in his first two seasons. That's the most ever in that span.

It's Up...It's Good!

More field goals were made in 2013 (863) than in any previous NFL season.

Fabulous Firsts

In beating the Cowboys, the Saints set an all-time NFL record with 40 first downs in the game.

Passing Fancy

QB Rating is a stat used to measure quarterback success. A record seven passers topped the 100.0 mark in 2013.

ENDING OF THE YEAR

If you left early during the December 8 Vikings–Ravens game, we feel really sorry for you. You missed one of the wildest final two minutes in NFL history. First, Baltimore scored with just over two minutes left to take the lead. Minnesota snatched it back 38 seconds later on a long run. The Ravens' **Jacoby Jones** then returned the kickoff for a score. A 79-yard TD pass gave the Vikings the lead once more. But there was time for one more drive. Baltimore's **Joe Flacco** made three completions; the final one was a TD pass with just nine seconds left. In all, five touchdowns were scored in 125 seconds!

More NFL News and Notes

2014 Pro Football Hall of Fame

A mixed group of offense, defense, and special teams players made up this year's class of NFL Hall of Famers.

Derrick Brooks
LB, Buccaneers

One of the best linebackers of the 2000s, he was the 2002 NFL Defensive Player of the Year and helped the Bucs win their only Super Bowl.

Ray Guy
P, Raiders

Called by many the best punter of all time, he starred for the Raiders for 14 years, helping them win three Super Bowls.

Claude Humphrey
LB, Falcons, Eagles

A pass-rushing specialist, Humphrey was part of the famous Falcons' Grits Blitz defense.

Walter Jones
T, Seahawks

He made the Pro Bowl in nine of his 12 seasons in Seattle and is considered one of the best tackles of the 2000s.

1 That's the number of punters in the Hall of Fame now that **Ray Guy** has been elected.

Andre Reed
WR, Bills, Redskins

A steady and dependable pass-catcher, Reed was part of the Bills' four AFC championship teams and was named to seven Pro Bowls.

Michael Strahan
DE, Giants

The single-season sacks leader (22.5 in 2001), he helped the Giants reach two Super Bowls. He has become a popular national TV talk-show host.

Aeneas Williams
CB, Cardinals, Rams

A shutdown corner who spent a lot of his career with poor teams, Williams had 55 career interceptions.

NFL DRAFT TOP TEN

Linemen on both sides of the ball were the most popular picks.

PICK	PLAYER/POSITION/SCHOOL	NFL TEAM
1	**Jadeveon Clowney**, DE, South Carolina	Texans
2	**Greg Robinson**, OT, Auburn	Rams
3	**Blake Bortles**, QB, Central Florida	Jaguars
4	**Sammy Watkins**, WR, Clemson	Bills
5	**Khalil Mack**, LB, Buffalo	Raiders
6	**Jake Matthews**, T, Texas A&M	Falcons
7	**Mike Evans**, WR, Texas A&M	Buccaneers
8	**Justin Gilbert**, CB, Oklahoma St.	Browns
9	**Anthony Barr**, LB, UCLA	Vikings
10	**Eric Ebron**, TE, North Carolina	Lions

A top pick with the commish.

DRAFT NOTES

* The Browns waited until the 22nd overall pick to choose "Johnny Football," as Texas A&M star **Johnny Manziel** is known. Many thought he would be drafted much higher.

* For the second year in a row—but only the second year since 1967—no running back went in the first round. **Bishop Sankey** of Washington was selected by the Titans with the 54th overall pick. It was the latest ever for the first rusher to be picked.

* Congrats to **Pat O'Donnell** of Miami. He was the only punter chosen (by the Bears in the sixth round).

* *USA Today* said the Browns, Rams, and Texans had the best drafts. They gave bad grades to the Panthers and Colts.

Arrivederci, Roma!

The Super Bowl has used Roman numerals to count its games since Super Bowl III (1968). In 2014, the NFL announced that for the 50th Super Bowl—which will be played near San Francisco in February 2016—it's "Arrivederci, Roma!" (That means "good-bye, Rome" in Italian.) The league will call the game Super Bowl 50, not Super Bowl L.

For the Record

Super Bowl Winners

GAME	SEASON	WINNING TEAM	LOSING TEAM	SCORE	SITE
XLVIII	2013	**Seattle**	Denver	43–8	New Jersey
XLVII	2012	**Baltimore**	San Francisco	34–31	New Orleans
XLVI	2011	**NY Giants**	New England	21–17	Indianapolis
XLV	2010	**Green Bay**	Pittsburgh	31–25	Dallas
XLIV	2009	**New Orleans**	Indianapolis	31–17	South Florida
XLIII	2008	**Pittsburgh**	Arizona	27–23	Tampa
XLII	2007	**NY Giants**	New England	17–14	Glendale, AZ
XLI	2006	**Indianapolis**	Chicago	29–17	South Florida
XL	2005	**Pittsburgh**	Seattle	21–10	Detroit
XXXIX	2004	**New England**	Philadelphia	24–21	Jacksonville
XXXVIII	2003	**New England**	Carolina	32–29	Houston
XXXVII	2002	**Tampa Bay**	Oakland	48–21	San Diego
XXXVI	2001	**New England**	St. Louis	20–17	New Orleans
XXXV	2000	**Baltimore**	NY Giants	34–7	Tampa
XXXIV	1999	**St. Louis**	Tennessee	23–16	Atlanta
XXXIII	1998	**Denver**	Atlanta	34–19	South Florida
XXXII	1997	**Denver**	Green Bay	31–24	San Diego
XXXI	1996	**Green Bay**	New England	35–21	New Orleans
XXX	1995	**Dallas**	Pittsburgh	27–17	Tempe, AZ
XXIX	1994	**San Francisco**	San Diego	49–26	South Florida
XXVIII	1993	**Dallas**	Buffalo	30–13	Atlanta
XXVII	1992	**Dallas**	Buffalo	52–17	Pasadena

GAME	SEASON	WINNING TEAM	LOSING TEAM	SCORE	SITE
XXVI	1991	**Washington**	Buffalo	**37-24**	Minneapolis
XXV	1990	**NY Giants**	Buffalo	**20-19**	Tampa
XXIV	1989	**San Francisco**	Denver	**55-10**	New Orleans
XXIII	1988	**San Francisco**	Cincinnati	**20-16**	South Florida
XXII	1987	**Washington**	Denver	**42-10**	San Diego
XXI	1986	**NY Giants**	Denver	**39-20**	Pasadena
XX	1985	**Chicago**	New England	**46-10**	New Orleans
XIX	1984	**San Francisco**	Miami	**38-16**	Stanford
XVIII	1983	**LA Raiders**	Washington	**38-9**	Tampa
XVII	1982	**Washington**	Miami	**27-17**	Pasadena
XVI	1981	**San Francisco**	Cincinnati	**26-21**	Pontiac, Mich.
XV	1980	**Oakland**	Philadelphia	**27-10**	New Orleans
XIV	1979	**Pittsburgh**	Los Angeles	**31-19**	Pasadena
XIII	1978	**Pittsburgh**	Dallas	**35-31**	Miami
XII	1977	**Dallas**	Denver	**27-10**	New Orleans
XI	1976	**Oakland**	Minnesota	**32-14**	Pasadena
X	1975	**Pittsburgh**	Dallas	**21-17**	Miami
IX	1974	**Pittsburgh**	Minnesota	**16-6**	New Orleans
VIII	1973	**Miami**	Minnesota	**24-7**	Houston
VII	1972	**Miami**	Washington	**14-7**	Los Angeles
VI	1971	**Dallas**	Miami	**24-3**	New Orleans
V	1970	**Baltimore**	Dallas	**16-13**	Miami
IV	1969	**Kansas City**	Minnesota	**23-7**	New Orleans
III	1968	**NY Jets**	Baltimore	**16-7**	Miami
II	1967	**Green Bay**	Oakland	**33-14**	Miami
I	1966	**Green Bay**	Kansas City	**35-10**	Los Angeles

PLAY OF THE YEAR . . . OR EVER!
*Auburn fans and coaches alike were jump-
ing for joy as Chris Davis headed for the end
zone. He was carrying a field goal missed by
Alabama, and 109 yards later, he scored with
no time left on the clock. The remarkable and
stunning play helped Auburn reach the BCS
championship game.*

COLLEGE FOOTBALL

Points Galore!

Baylor went on a point-scoring binge!

Right up to the final seconds, the 2013 college football season had enough suspense to keep fans all over the country on the edge of their seats. The national championship wasn't decided until Florida State scored a touchdown in the final seconds to beat Auburn 34–31 in the BCS title game.

The back-and-forth championship game was a fitting end to a wild-and-woolly year in which the name of the game was putting points on the scoreboard. The spread offense, the no-huddle, the hurry-up, the zone-read, the pistol—offensive coordinators around the country used dozens of formations and gimmicks. College football scores looked like basketball scores!

FINAL 2013 AP TOP 10

1. **Florida State**
2. **Auburn**
3. **Michigan State**
4. **South Carolina**
5. **Missouri**
6. **Oklahoma**
7. **Alabama**
8. **Clemson**
9. **Oregon**
10. **Central Florida**

AWARD WINNERS

HEISMAN TROPHY (BEST PLAYER)
DAVEY O'BRIEN AWARD (QUARTERBACK)
Jameis Winston
Florida State

CHUCK BEDNARIK AWARD (DEFENSIVE PLAYER)
BRONKO NAGURSKI AWARD (DEFENSIVE PLAYER)
OUTLAND TROPHY (INTERIOR LINEMAN)
VINCE LOMBARDI AWARD (LINEMAN)
Aaron Donald
Pittsburgh

DOAK WALKER AWARD (RUNNING BACK)
Andre Williams
Boston College

FRED BILETNIKOFF AWARD (WIDE RECEIVER)
Brandin Cooks
Oregon State

JOHN MACKEY AWARD (TIGHT END)
Austin Seferian-Jenkins
Washington

DICK BUTKUS AWARD (LINEBACKER)
C.J. Mosley
Alabama

LOU GROZA AWARD (KICKER)
Roberto Aguayo
Florida State

Aaron Donald cleaned up the defensive honors.

Take Baylor, for instance. The Bears opened the season by scoring 69 points in a victory over Wofford. Then they scored 70, 70, and 73 points in their next three games. By season's end, they had averaged more than 50 points and 600 total yards while winning a school-record 11 games. National-champion Florida State averaged 51.6 points per game and scored more than 50 points seven times, including a school-record 80 points against Idaho! No. 2 Auburn averaged 39.5 points per game.

It looked like there's no end in sight to the offensive explosion as teams scrambled to keep up with their rivals. But don't tell that to Michigan State. The Spartans went retro with a conservative offense and a hard-hitting defense to win their last 10 games, including the Rose Bowl, in the 2013 season. They finished the season ranked No. 3 in the nation! The title game (page 45) kept the scoring going.

2013 BCS Bowl Games

BCS NATIONAL CHAMPIONSHIP GAME

Florida State 34, Auburn 31

The Seminoles rallied to win the national championship on a touchdown pass in the final seconds of the game.

Roses for champion Michigan State.

ROSE BOWL

Michigan State 24, Stanford 20

In a season dominated by offense, these two defensive stalwarts slugged it out in the 100th Rose Bowl Game in Pasadena.

SUGAR BOWL

Oklahoma 45, Alabama 31

Sooners freshman **Trevor Knight** passed for 4 touchdowns to steal the headlines from outgoing Crimson Tide QB **AJ McCarron**.

FIESTA BOWL

Central Florida 52, Baylor 42

These two offensive juggernauts combined for 1,106 yards and 13 touchdowns in the highest-scoring Fiesta Bowl ever.

ORANGE BOWL

Clemson 40, Ohio State 35

Quarterback **Tajh Boyd** accounted for 505 yards and 6 touchdowns passing and rushing as the Tigers won a BCS game for the first time.

OTHER BOWLS

There were 35 bowl games played in 2013–14. Here are some other highlights.

SUN BOWL: UCLA showed the West was strong with a big win over Virginia Tech.

COTTON BOWL: SEC runnerup Missouri got a big W by defeating Oklahoma State.

PINSTRIPE BOWL: Notre Dame won its 16th all-time bowl game by defeating Rutgers at Yankee Stadium!

FSU=No. 1!
2013 BCS Championship

The final BCS National Championship Game (see page 51) was also one of the best. The top-ranked Florida State Seminoles won their first national championship since 1999 by outlasting No. 2 Auburn 34–31 in the title game in Pasadena, California. The winning score came on sensational freshman quarterback **Jameis Winston's** 2-yard touchdown pass to **Kelvin Benjamin** with just 13 seconds left.

All season long, Auburn looked like a team of destiny. The Tigers won a game on a TD pass with 10 seconds left. They won another game on a 73-yard touchdown pass with 25 seconds left when the ball bounced off a defender's hands right to their wide receiver! And they beat Alabama on a 109-yard return—the longest play possible in football—of a missed field goal as time ran out.

It looked as if the BCS National Championship Game would be another dramatic win for Auburn when the Tigers took a 31–27 lead on **Tre Mason's** 37-yard touchdown run with just 1:19 remaining. The undefeated Seminoles weren't used to being behind. They won their first 13 games by an average of 42 points. But Winston, who set NCAA freshman records with 4,047 yards and 40 touchdowns passing, calmly rallied his team. From the 20-yard line, he completed an 8-yard pass to **Rashard Greene**, and then a 49-yard strike to Greene. Suddenly, Florida State was at Auburn's 23-yard line. Five plays later, the Seminoles scored the winning touchdown to become national champs.

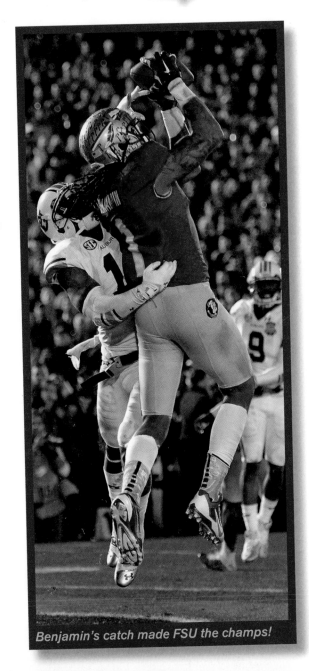

Benjamin's catch made FSU the champs!

2013 Highlights

Alabama's Revenge

The most hyped game of the 2013 season was No. 1-ranked Alabama's trip to No. 6 Texas A&M in Week 3. Alabama was coming off back-to-back national championships, but quarterback **Johnny Manziel**—"Johnny Football"—and the Aggies had upset the Crimson Tide in Alabama in 2012. For once, the game lived up to the hype. Manziel passed for 464 yards and five touchdowns. Unfortunately, another of his passes went for a touchdown the other way. Thanks to that big defensive play and four TD passes by **AJ McCarron**, Alabama won, 49–42.

Tough Road Trip

USC's Pac-12 title hopes were dashed by a pair of early season losses, including a 62–41 drubbing at Arizona State on September 28. That road trip got even worse for head coach **Lane Kiffin**. After the team's plane landed in Los Angeles, he was told he had been fired! Things did get better for the Trojans, who were re-energized under interim coach Ed Orgeron. USC went on to win 10 games, including an upset of fifth-ranked Stanford and a victory over No. 20 Fresno State in the Las Vegas Bowl. Former Washington coach **Steve Sarkisian** took over as the Trojans' head man going into 2014.

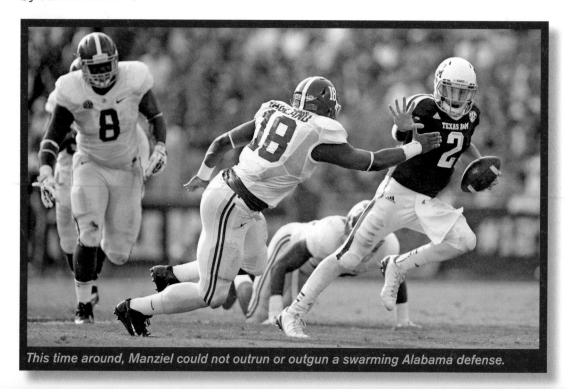

This time around, Manziel could not outrun or outgun a swarming Alabama defense.

The Higher They're Ranked...

. . . the harder they fall. Week 8 was a rough week for the nation's top-rated teams. Nine of the Associated Press' top 20 teams—including Nos. 3, 6, 7, 8, 9, and 11—all lost. The weekend started when unranked Central Florida stunned undefeated Louisville 38–35 on Friday night on a touchdown with 23 seconds left. But the biggest game was No. 5 Florida State's 51–14 defeat of Clemson on the road on Saturday. That put the Seminoles squarely in the national-title talk, and ended the Tigers' hopes.

Thursday Night Football

There's nothing quite as good as a Saturday afternoon of college football . . . unless it's a Thursday night? That was the biggest night of Week 11, at least, when a pair of huge games kicked off under the lights. First, No. 6 Baylor passed its first major test of the season by thumping No. 12 Oklahoma 41–12. Then No. 5 Stanford built a 26–0 early in the fourth quarter against visiting Oregon and held off the second-ranked Ducks 26–20.

Central Florida won on an upset weekend.

Dream Day

December 7, 2013, was a dream day for college football fans, with several games shaping the national-championship picture. Top-ranked and undefeated Florida State knew it would go to the BCS title game with a win over Duke in the ACC Championship Game. The Seminoles left no doubt with a 45–7 rout. Next in line was 12–0 Ohio State, but when the Buckeyes lost to Michigan State 34–24, the door was open for No. 3 Auburn. The Tigers rolled past Missouri 59–42 with a dominating offensive performance in the Southeastern Conference title game. Michigan State headed to the Rose Bowl against Stanford, which hammered Arizona State 38–14 to win the Pac-12 championship.

More 2013 Highlights

Small school, big record for McKoy.

it. With a bunch of linemen in the game to block for the field-goal try, Alabama had nobody that could keep up with the speedy Davis, who took off down the left sideline. He raced 109 yards to the end zone to win the game for Auburn 34–28 and send the hometown fans at Jordan-Hare Stadium into a frenzy.

Tip Drill

Georgia had a late-season victory over Auburn right at its fingertips— literally!—before it got away. The Bulldogs rallied from a 20-point deficit in the fourth quarter to take a 38–37 lead. Then Auburn faced fourth-and-18 at its 27-yard line with 36 seconds left. Tigers quarterback **Nick Marshall** heaved a long pass downfield. Two Georgia players leaped to knock it down. One got his hand on the ball, but instead of down, it popped up . . . right into the hands of Tigers wide receiver **Ricardo Louis**. He raced to the end zone to complete an incredible 73-yard touchdown for a 43–38 win.

Instant Classic

The annual Iron Bowl between Alabama and Auburn already had been a good one, with great back-and-forth action. With the score tied 28–28 and one second left, the Crimson Tide lined up for a potential game-winning, 57-yard field-goal try. Then the game became one of the all-time greats.

Adam Griffith's long kick fell just short of the goalposts. Tigers return man **Chris Davis**, who was standing near the back line of the end zone, caught

Two-Way Star

UCLA linebacker **Myles Jack** made a big impact in his freshman season—by running the football. With the Bruins hurt by injuries, Jack played offense and defense, rushing for 120 yards and 2 touchdowns and making 8 tackles and recovering a fumble in a 31–26 victory over Arizona. The next week, Jack ran for 4 touchdowns in a 41–31 victory over Washington. Pretty good results for a guy who usually makes tackles, not avoids them!

Record Rusher

Western Connecticut running back **Octavias McKoy** had a pretty good season—in one afternoon! Against Worcester State, McKoy set an NCAA all-division record when he rushed for 455 yards (and scored 5 touchdowns) in the Division III Colonials' 55–35 victory. He carried 43 times, and scored on runs of 15, 1, 41, 53, and 71 yards. And, in case you're wondering, McKoy really did have a pretty good season. He finished the year with 1,833 yards and 28 touchdowns.

50,291,275

That's how many fans attended at least one NCAA football game in 2013, an all-time record. How many did you attend?

Working Overtime

Penn State needed four overtimes to beat Michigan 43–40, handing the Wolverines their first loss after five wins to open the season. For both teams, it was the longest game in school history. Michigan's **Brendan Gibbons** kicked 4 field goals, but he also missed 3 potential winning tries at the end of regulation and in overtime. The Nittany Lions' **Bill Belton** ran 2 yards for the winning touchdown in the fourth extra session.

Football players all used to play offense and defense. Myles Jack went "old school" in 2013.

Conference Champs

AMERICAN ATHLETIC:
CENTRAL FLORIDA

Louisville was the preseason favorite and a sleeper pick for the national championship, but Central Florida stunned the Cardinals 38–35 early in the conference season and went on to win the inaugural American Athletic championship. The Knights finished the year 12–1.

QB Anthony Boone led Duke to one of its best seasons ever.

> **❝He keeps everyone calm when the tight situations come down to the wire. We wouldn't want anyone in the huddle other than him.❞**
>
> — UCF RECEIVER J.J. WORTON
> ON HIS QUARTERBACK, BLAKE BORTLES

ATLANTIC COAST:
FLORIDA STATE

Duke was one of the storybook teams of 2013: The Blue Devils won 10 games in a season for the first time in 101 years of playing football. They were no match for Florida State in the ACC title game, though, as the Seminoles rolled to a 45–7 victory.

BIG TEN:
MICHIGAN STATE

Ohio State was 12–0 and needed only a victory over Michigan State in the Big Ten Championship Game to play for the BCS championship. But the Spartans rallied for a 34–24 victory, then went on to win the Rose Bowl on New Year's Day.

BIG 12:
BAYLOR

High-scoring Baylor forged one of the best seasons in school history while winning the Big 12 for the first time. The Bears led the nation in points per game

Auburn celebrated after knocking off Missouri, its surprise SEC title game opponent.

and opened the season with nine consecutive wins before settling for an 11–2 record.

PAC-12:
STANFORD

Stanford emerged as the winner of the rugged Pac-12 North in large part because of its 26–20 victory over No. 2-ranked Oregon on November 7. Then the Cardinal won their second consecutive conference championship by routing Arizona State in the title game.

SOUTHEASTERN:
AUBURN

Little was expected of Auburn after the team failed to win a conference game in 2012. But first-year head coach **Gus Malzahn** guided the Tigers to a series of stirring victories and a berth in the BCS National Championship Game.

A LOOK AHEAD
PLAYOFF TIME

For all those fans who have been clamoring for a playoff, the time has finally come. College football will feature its first four-team playoff for the 2014 season. Here's how it works: Six major bowls (Rose, Sugar, Orange, Cotton, Fiesta, and Peach) will be played on New Year's Eve and New Year's Day each season. Two of those bowls will serve as national semifinals. (The semifinals will rotate bowls each year; in the 2014 season, it will be the Rose and Sugar Bowls.) The winners of the two semifinal games will meet in the championship game at a different site each year, kind of like the Super Bowl. In the 2014 season, the game will be played on January 12, 2015, in Arlington, Texas.

COLLEGE FOOTBALL PLAYOFF

@CFBPLAYOFF

We're No. 1!

These are the teams that have finished at the top of the Associated Press's final rankings since the poll was first introduced in 1936.

SEASON	TEAM	RECORD	SEASON	TEAM	RECORD
2013	Florida State	14–0	1974	Oklahoma	11–0
2012	Alabama	13–1	1973	Notre Dame	11–0
2011	Alabama	12–1	1972	USC	12–0
2010	Auburn	14–0	1971	Nebraska	13–0
2009	Alabama	14–0	1970	Nebraska	11–0–1
2008	Florida	13–1	1969	Texas	11–0
2007	LSU	12–2	1968	Ohio State	10–0
2006	Florida	13–1	1967	USC	10–1
2005	Texas	13–0	1966	Notre Dame	9–0–1
2004	USC	13–0	1965	Alabama	9–1–1
2003	USC	12–1	1964	Alabama	10–1
2002	Ohio State	14–0	1963	Texas	11–0
2001	Miami	12–0	1962	USC	11–0
2000	Oklahoma	13–0	1961	Alabama	11–0
1999	Florida State	12–0	1960	Minnesota	8–2
1998	Tennessee	13–0	1959	Syracuse	11–0
1997	Michigan	12–0	1958	LSU	11–0
1996	Florida	12–1	1957	Auburn	10–0
1995	Nebraska	12–0	1956	Oklahoma	10–0
1994	Nebraska	13–0	1955	Oklahoma	11–0
1993	Florida State	12–1	1954	Ohio State	10–0
1992	Alabama	13–0	1953	Maryland	10–1
1991	Miami	12–0	1952	Michigan State	9–0
1990	Colorado	11–1–1	1951	Tennessee	10–1
1989	Miami	11–1	1950	Oklahoma	10–1
1988	Notre Dame	12–0	1949	Notre Dame	10–0
1987	Miami	12–0	1948	Michigan	9–0
1986	Penn State	12–0	1947	Notre Dame	9–0
1985	Oklahoma	11–1	1946	Notre Dame	8–0–1
1984	Brigham Young	13–0	1945	Army	9–0
1983	Miami	11–1	1944	Army	9–0
1982	Penn State	11–1	1943	Notre Dame	9–1
1981	Clemson	12–0	1942	Ohio State	9–1
1980	Georgia	12–0	1941	Minnesota	8–0
1979	Alabama	12–0	1940	Minnesota	8–0
1978	Alabama	11–1	1939	Texas A&M	11–0
1977	Notre Dame	11–1	1938	Texas Christian	11–0
1976	Pittsburgh	12–0	1937	Pittsburgh	9–0–1
1975	Oklahoma	11–1	1936	Minnesota	7–1

BOWL CHAMPIONSHIP SERIES
NATIONAL CHAMPIONSHIP GAMES

College football (at its highest level) is one of the few sports that doesn't have an on-field playoff to determine its champion. In the 1998 season, the NCAA introduced the Bowl Championship Series (BCS), which pits the top two teams in the title game according to a complicated formula. The 2013 season was the last for the BCS, however, and a new four-team final playoff will be held starting with the 2014 season.

SEASON	SCORE	SITE
2013	Florida State 34, Auburn 31	PASADENA, CA
2012	Alabama 42, Notre Dame 14	MIAMI, FL
2011	Alabama 21, LSU 0	NEW ORLEANS, LA
2010	Auburn 22, Oregon 19	GLENDALE, AZ
2009	Alabama 37, Texas 21	PASADENA, CA
2008	Florida 24, Oklahoma 14	MIAMI, FL
2007	LSU 38, Ohio State 24	NEW ORLEANS, LA
2006	Florida 41, Ohio State 14	GLENDALE, AZ
2005	Texas 41, USC 38	PASADENA, CA
2004	USC 55, Oklahoma 19	MIAMI, FL
2003	LSU 21, Oklahoma 14	NEW ORLEANS, LA
2002	Ohio State 31, Miami 24	TEMPE, AZ
2001	Miami 37, Nebraska 14	PASADENA, CA
2000	Oklahoma 13, Florida State 2	MIAMI, FL
1999	Florida State 46, Virginia Tech 29	NEW ORLEANS, LA
1998	Tennessee 23, Florida State 16	TEMPE, AZ

2014 WINTER OLYMPICS

GOLDEN GIRL!
US slalom skier Mikaela Shiffrin became the youngest Alpine skiing gold medalist ever. Only 18 years old, she overcame huge pressure and a tough field of opponents to win. Her gold medal was a big highlight for the American team in the 2014 Winter Olympics in Sochi, Russia.

"Russian" to Gold!

S ochi, Russia, home of the 2014 Winter Olympics, is normally a summer resort. Russians head there to swim in the Black Sea and hang out at the beach. So . . . Winter Olympics? Turns out a summer resort (and its nearby snow-covered mountains!) is a pretty good place to have the Games. Over two weeks, palm trees waved outside the skating arenas near the water, while snow fell on gold medalists in the mountains.

The host nation of Russia ended up with the most medals. Of course, they enjoyed a homefield advantage! US athletes did very well, too, taking home medals in skiing, bobsledding, and skating.

But it was in the "action" sports in which Americans had the most success. Snowboarding, sno-cross, aerials, moguls, and other ripped-from-the-X-Games sports sent more Americans to the top of the medal stand than any other activity.

Sage Kotsenburg was a surprised (and happy) winner!

33

The host nation of Russia led the final medals standings with 13 gold, 11 silver, and nine bronze. For a list of the top 10 nations, see page 63.

White and Davis danced to gold for the US.

A hang-loose dude from Idaho won the first medal of the Games for the US. In the snowboard slopestyle event, **Sage Kotsenburg** did a trick he had never tried before in competition! He nailed it and won gold. That kicked off an action-sports romp. **Jamie Anderson** won the women's snowboard slopestyle. **Kaitlyn Farrington** was a surprise champ in the women's snowboard halfpipe. The men's version of that event saw disappointment for US star **Shaun White**. The two-time defending champ battled a wrist injury and wound up fourth, out of the medal race. But in slopestyle skiing, red, white, and blue grabbed gold, silver, and bronze. **Joss Christensen**, **Gus Kenworthy**, and **Nick Goepper** swept those medals in this new Olympic event.

In Alpine skiing, Americans had several early disappointments. Superstar **Lindsey Vonn** hurt her knee and could not even compete. Favorites **Bode Miller** and **Julia Mancuso** did not earn medals in downhill. But the team rebounded in later events. Miller became the oldest medalist ever on the slopes with a bronze in super giant slalom. **Andrew Weibrecht** had silver in the same event. Then **Ted Ligety** earned gold in the

❝She was really confident. She said, 'I'm going to win. I'm the world champion, and I'm going to do it.'❞ — SHIFFRIN'S COACH, ROLAND PFEIFER

giant slalom. The Alpine team's recovery was wrapped up when **Mikaela Shiffrin**, 18, won the gold in the slalom. She was the youngest ski-race winner in Olympic history!

The hockey tournament didn't end well for the US (page 60) but another ice team brought home gold. The US couple **Charlie White** and **Meryl Davis** won their first gold medal in ice dancing. Read about more American medalists on page 58. Plus, see the complete gold-medalist list on page 62.

USA! USA!

Here are more American highlights from the 2014 Winter Games.

❋ Good Ending: Veteran skeleton racer Noelle Pikus-Pace earned silver and then retired from her sport!

❋ Golden Dreams: A few months after Maddie Bowman's grandmother had a dream that Maddie would win at the Olympics . . . Maddie did! She won the women's halfpipe skiing competition. She was the youngest skier in the final round.

▲ Bobbing for Gold: The last time the US won a medal in two-man bobsled, Dwight Eisenhower was president and the Dodgers and Giants played in New York City! So when Steven Holcomb and Steven Langton rode their sled to a bronze-medal finish in Sochi, it broke a 62-year drought! Holcomb had to overcome a calf injury. But this is nothing new for him: He won gold in 2010 in the four-man event, the first US medal there since 1948! In the two-woman race, Elana Meyers and Lauryn Williams missed gold in their event by only one-tenth of a second.

❋ Comeback: After not medaling in the downhill or the Super-G, veteran racer Julia Mancuso bounced back to win her fourth career Olympic medal, a bronze in the super combined.

❋ Golden Necklace: Ski halfpipe gold medal winner David Wise told reporters that his young daughter would probably ask him for his gold medal to add to her jewelry collection!

Ice-skating

Figure skating is always one of the most popular events in the Olympics. Here are the key results.

WOMEN'S SINGLES:

Though some of her rivals grumbled about the scoring, Adelina Sotnikova (right) enjoyed the cheers of her fellow Russians when she earned the gold. She overcame defending champion Yuna Kim of South Korea. Social media erupted afterward to claim that Kim had been robbed. But skating experts pointed to Sotnikova's long list of jumps overcoming Kim's more fluid skating.

MEN'S:

Japan's Yuzuru Hanyu began the men's short program as an unheralded threat in a field full of champions. But one by one, the others fell or did not perform well. Then Hanyu set a world record with his short program. In the free skate, those champions just couldn't catch the young man from Japan. Even though he fell twice, his score held up and he earned his first gold medal.

PAIRS:

After setting a world record in the short program, Tatiana Volosozhar and Maxim Trankov brought Russia another gold in pairs skating. Another Russian pair earned the silver medal.

Gracie Gold helped the US earn a bronze medal in the new team figure skating event. Russia won the gold.

O Canada!

Winter sports are a big deal in Canada, home to thousands of square miles of ice and snow. Here are some of the Olympics highlights for the folks with the maple-leaf flag.

Family Ties

Three sisters from Canada made the finals of the women's moguls, so you had to figure they had a chance for a medal. They did better than that: **Justine** and **Chloe Dufour-Lapointe** won gold and silver, knocking off the favored American champion **Hannah Kearney** along the way.

Curling Crazy!

In Canada, curling is like bowling in America: Lots of people do it, but only a few do it really, really well. At the Olympics, Canada showed just how good they are at this sport, which is like shuffleboard on ice. Both the men's and women's team earned gold medals. The women beat Sweden, while the men overcame Great Britain.

◀Hockey Night in Canada Times Two!

In two dramatic games against their American archrivals, Canada's ice hockey teams were victorious. First, the women's team trailed by two goals with less than four minutes to go in the final. They struck back with two goals to tie and then won on **Marie-Philip Poulin's** goal in overtime to win the gold. The men's team made a second-period goal stand up in the semifinal against the high-scoring US team and won 1-0. The Canadian men then beat Sweden for their second straight gold medal.

A World of Stars

Twenty-six different nations won at least one medal in Sochi. Here are some of the highlights from those victories.

ULTIMATE WINNERS: Ole Einar Bjoerndalen of Norway won the 10-kilometer biathlon as well as gold in a biathlon relay. The medals gave him 13 for his amazing career, the most ever by an athlete in Winter Games history. Marit Bjoergen, also from Norway, equaled the top women's winner ever with her 10th cross-country medal.

NEW GOLD: For the first time, women took part in ski jumping in the Olympics. Carina Vogt of Germany won. Jessica Jerome, in tenth place, was the highest American finisher.

DOWN THE CHUTE: The luge relay was another new event for 2014. Each nation sent out a man, a woman, and a men's team. Their combined times determined the winner. The team from Germany won the first gold in this event.

▲ DUTCH SPEEDSTERS: Athletes from the Netherlands dominated speedskating, winning an amazing 23 medals. Their eight golds were a record, while their medal total was 10 more than all the other nations combined. Ireen Wust won five medals, the most of any athlete at these Games.

PARALYMPICS 2014

A few weeks after the Winter Olympics, the Winter Paralympics were held in the same venues in Sochi. Nearly 700 disabled athletes from 45 countries took part in alpine and cross-country skiing, biathlon, sledge hockey, and wheelchair curling. The athletes used special gear to race, ski, skate, and compete, demonstrating the theme of the Paralympics: Nothing is impossible. Host nation Russia led the way with 30 gold medals.

Olympic Lists

US MEDALISTS

GOLD MEDALS

Men's Giant Slalom
Ted Ligety

Ice Dancing
Meryl Davis and Charlie White

Men's Ski Slopestyle
Joss Christensen

Women's Snowboard Halfpipe
Kaitlyn Farrington

Women's Snowboard Slopestyle
Jamie Anderson

Men's Snowboard Slopestyle
Sage Kotsenburg

Women's Ski Halfpipe
Maddie Bowman

Women's Slalom
Mikaela Shiffrin

Men's Ski Halfpipe
David Wise

SILVER MEDALS

Speedskating
Men's 5,000-Meter Relay

Women's Ice Hockey

Women's Two-Person Bobsled

Women's Ski Slopestyle
Devin Logan

Men's Ski Slopestyle
Gus Kenworthy

Men's Super G
Andrew Weibrecht

Women's Skeleton
Noelle Pikus-Pace

BRONZE MEDALS

Women's Two-Person Bobsled

Team Figure Skating

Men's Bobsled/Two-Man

Men's Four-Man Bobsled

Snowboard, Women's Halfpipe
Kelly Clark

Women's Luge
Erin Hamlin

Skiing, Women's Super Combined
Julia Mancuso

Freestyle Skiing, Women's Moguls
Hannah Kearney

Freestyle Skiing, Men's Slopestyle
Nick Goepper

Snowboard, Men's Snowboard Cross
Alex Deibold

Skiing, Men's Super-G
Bode Miller

Men's Skeleton
Matt Antoine

2014 WINTER OLYMPICS FINAL MEDAL RESULTS

COUNTRY	GOLD	SILVER	BRONZE	TOTAL
RUSSIA	13	11	9	33
UNITED STATES	9	7	12	28
NORWAY	11	5	10	26
CANADA	10	10	5	25
NETHERLANDS	8	7	9	24
GERMANY	8	6	5	19
AUSTRIA	4	8	5	17
FRANCE	4	4	7	15
SWEDEN	2	7	6	15
SWITZERLAND	6	3	2	11

 # CANADIAN GOLD

Here are Canada's 10 gold medals.

WOMEN'S MOGULS
Justine Dufour-Lapointe

MEN'S MOGULS
Alex Bilodeaur

MEN'S 1,500-METER SHORT-TRACK SPEEDSKATING
Charles Hamelin

WOMEN'S SKI SLOPESTYLE
Dara Howell

WOMEN'S SKI CROSS
Marielle Thompson

WOMEN'S TWO-PERSON BOBSLED

WOMEN'S CURLING

MEN'S CURLING

WOMEN'S ICE HOCKEY

MEN'S ICE HOCKEY

SOCCER

WORLD CUP WINNER!
Germany's Mario Götze has a front-row seat to watch his goal sail past Argentina's Sergio Romero. Götze's shot, in the 113th minute of the 2014 World Cup final, was the only one of the game and made Germany a four-time champion.

World Cup!

After more than two years of qualifying games among more than 200 nations, the World Cup finally came down to 32 teams in Brazil. They came from six continents, and so did the fans, more than 3.4 million of them. Over a month of competition, those fans—and billions more around the world—watched some very entertaining soccer. There were stunning goals, big upsets, surprise collapses, and every emotion you can think of. For so many people, soccer is more than just a game—it is a vital part of their lives.

The eight groups of four teams battled for more than two weeks. Each game, each goal, each kick was watched eagerly by fans "back home." The team watched by most was Brazil, playing in front of its home fans. They won their first game over Croatia, but gave up an own goal. They could not score against Mexico and tied 0–0. They whomped Cameroon, but then struggled against

Brazil and its soccer-happy fans put on a great World Cup show for people around the world.

Chile in the round of 16. In barely beating Colombia, they lost star striker Neymar to a back injury. Then came their epic collapse against Germany (see page 70).

Another South American team did unexpectedly well. Colombia scored 9 goals in the first three games, second behind the Netherlands. Its young forward **James** (pronounced "HA-mehs") **Rodriguez** was a breakout star. Two African countries moved on, Nigeria and Algeria.

Fans in the US got their biggest shock when America's all-time leading scorer, **Landon Donovan**, was left off the team by coach **Jürgen Klinsmann**. That snub got more attention than some of the games from US sports fans. But it was forgotten when the Americans got a little help to make it into the final 16 (see page 69).

After the group stage was over, some unexpected teams were heading home. While the United States squeaked into the final 16, powerhouses including England, Spain, and Italy were done. England, in fact, earned only one point, its worst World Cup since 1958.

Heading into the "knockout" rounds, most experts still looked at the traditional favorites to make it far: Germany, Brazil, Argentina, the Netherlands. And that's exactly how the semifinals ended up. But there were thrills along the way. The Netherlands had to score two goals in the final two minutes to escape a second-round game against Mexico. Then they were taken to penalty kicks by the surprising Costa Rica team. Brazil had to go to penalty kicks against Chile to advance. Even Germany fell behind to Algeria before rallying to continue its climb to the final.

But the upsets ended at that point. Germany and Argentina made it to the final game, and put on an entertaining final that turned on one key play. Check out the action on page 71.

WOW!

Robin van Persie had what turned out to be the best goal of the tournament in the Netherlands' opening game. His flying header, off a perfect curling, 40-yard cross, looped in over Iker Casillas of Spain. Netherlands won 5–1, a bit of revenge for losing to Spain in the 2010 World Cup Final.

World Cup
Early-Round Action

Central American Surprise

Costa Rica has only 4.8 million residents, one of the smallest countries in the World Cup. All of the Costa Ricans were happy for most of the World Cup. Their players, known as the Ticos, did not lose a game except in penalties. They allowed only two goals in the run of play, helped by their amazing goalie **Keylor Navas**. They were the "little guys" in a round of 16 dominated by world soccer powers.

Suarez Eats Italian?

Uruguay striker **Luis Suarez** is one of the world's most exciting scorers. He's also one of the weirdest. For the third time in his career, he was fined and suspended after biting an opponent! Following his team's game against

Navas helped Costa Rica to big wins.

Italy, World Cup officials watched the video of Suarez chomping on the shoulder of an Italian player. Then they kicked him out of the World Cup and all world soccer for nine months.

QUICK KICKS

※ Australia nearly upset the Netherlands, helped in part by **Tim Cahill**'s amazing left-footed volley that some called the goal of the tournament.

※ Mexican goalie **Guillermo Ochoa** became a national hero after shutting out mighty Brazil. He made numerous saves, several on point-blank shots.

※ Belgium was a surprise as one of the high seeds, but they came through. They won their group and showed some great attacking soccer.

◀◀◀ Great players make great goals. **Lionel Messi** showed that with this perfect free-kick goal against Nigeria, one of his four scores in the World Cup.

World Cup
Team USA

GAME 1

The World Cup could not have started better for the Americans. Only 30 seconds into their opening game against Ghana, **Clint Dempsey** scored. It was a shocking beginning, and it gave the US players great confidence. However, they allowed Ghana to tie the game in the 82nd minute. Another shock came four minutes later. US defender **John Brooks** headed in a corner kick and the US opened the World Cup with a huge win.

GAME 2

With less than 30 seconds to go, the US held a 2–1 lead over powerful Portugal. **Jermaine Jones** had tied the score with a crushing drive, and **Dempsey** had knocked in the go-ahead goal. But Portugal never gave up. **Cristiano Ronaldo** made a perfect cross to **Varela**. His header tied the game seconds before the final whistle. The tie was a point for the US, but it should have been a win.

Dempsey has the scoring touch for the US team.

GAME 3

If the US beat Germany, they'd go through. They would also make it to the next round if Portugal did not win by enough goals. As it turned out, the Americans needed the help. Though they played well, they lost to Germany 1–0. But Portugal won only 2-1, so with four points in three games, the US was one of 16 World Cup finalists.

ROUND OF 16

US goalie **Tim Howard** became an international sensation with his performance in this must-win match against Belgium. The keeper made a World Cup–record 16 saves, many of them diving, sprawling, and dramatic. He kept the US in the game, taking the game scoreless into overtime. But the US finally cracked and Belgium scored twice in the extra periods. The US got a late goal to make it closer, but even with the great Howard in action, the US was done in the Cup, losing 2–1.

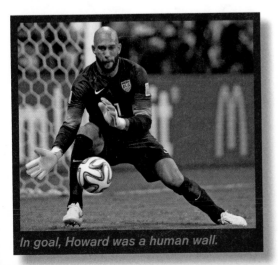

In goal, Howard was a human wall.

World Cup! Semifinals

SEMIFINAL 1
Simply Shocking

World soccer fans could not believe what they were seeing during the Brazil-Germany semifinal match. Yes, Brazil had lost two key players. But what happened was literally an all-time first. Brazil played like a youth-league team, while Germany was perfect. They beat the Brazilians by a stunning 7–1 score. It was the most goals ever given up by a Brazilian team and their worst World Cup loss ever. In fact, Brazil had never given up five goals in an entire World Cup, let alone one game. That it came in front of their home fans led to a lot of tears for the team in yellow.

SEMIFINAL 2
A New Hero for Argentina

Lionel Messi is regarded as the best player in the world, but Argentina depended on another player to send them to the World Cup final. Against the Netherlands, Messi was bottled up by an aggressive Dutch defense. But Argentina's D kept the powerful Dutch team, led by **Arjen Robben** and **Robin van Persie**, from scoring. After 120 minutes with no goals, it went to penalty kicks. And the new hero for the South Americans? That was Argentina goalie **Sergio Romero**, who stopped two Dutch PKs to win the game.

NEW SCORING CHAMP

In Germany's rout of Brazil, forward **Miroslav Klose** had the second goal. That gave him 16 for his World Cup career—he has now played in four—and set a new career record. He had scored earlier in the tournament to tie Brazil's **Ronaldo**.

World Cup! Final

As more than a billion people tuned in, Germany faced Argentina in the World Cup final. The magic of **Lionel Messi** against the powerful team play of the Germans. The range of German goalie **Manuel Neuer** or the defensive wall of the Argentines. Would the South American team have home-continent advantage? Or would the Germans become the first Europeans to win in the other hemisphere?

CHAMPIONS
2014 FIFA World Cup

Each team had chances. Argentina's **Gonzalo Higuain** missed a clear shot and German defender **Jerome Boateng** made a big save on the line. Messi missed a good chance early in the second half. **Klose** missed a header for Germany, while **Mehmet Ozil** also whipped a shot past the post. But it was scoreless after 90 minutes.

Extra time was nearing the end when Germany made one more rush downfield. **André Schürrle** lofted a pass toward the Argentine goal. Forward **Mario Götze** made a perfect chest pass to himself, and slammed a volley past **Romero**. The goal, in the 113th minute, was one of the latest game-winners in Cup history.

The 1–0 victory gave Germany its fourth World Cup and first since 1990. It now trails only Brazil, which has six world titles.

2014 WORLD CUP AWARDS

GOLDEN BALL
(best player in tournament)
Lionel Messi, Argentina

GOLDEN GLOVES
(best goalie)
Manuel Neuer, Germany

GOLDEN BOOT
(highest scorer)
James Rodriguez,
Colombia, 6 goals

YOUNG PLAYER AWARD
(best player born 1993 or after)
Paul Progba, France

FAIR PLAY AWARD
(least fouls among final 16)
Colombia

Other Soccer News

MLS CUP

The 2013 MLS Cup seemed like the game that would never end. For fans sitting in the 22-degree weather, it seemed even more endless. Oddly, the game came down to a player who had never taken a penalty kick in his soccer career! Sporting Kansas City and Real Salt Lake played to a 1–1 tie after 120 minutes that included a half-hour of extra time. The penalty-kick shootout went on for round after round. Each team's goalie made clutch saves, while players on both sides missed chances to wrap it up. With the score in penalties tied at 6–6, KC defender **Aurelien Collin** took his turn. He buried the shot and said afterward,

MLS GROWS!

In 2015, Major League Soccer welcomes two new teams. New York City FC kicks off, looking to create a rivalry with the New York Red Bulls across the river. In Orlando, superstar **David Beckham** is a part-owner of the Orlando City Soccer Club that will start in 2015 as well. In 2017, look for another new MLS team to start in Atlanta.

"I hope I never have to take another one again!" However, it was then up to KC's star goalie, **Jimmy Neilsen**, to stop **Lovel Palmer**'s shot to seal the title. It was the first MLS championship for KC since 2000.

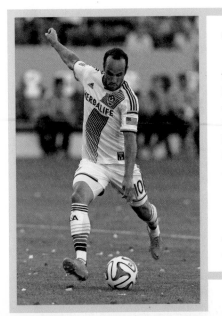

Take That, Coach!

Landon Donovan of the LA Galaxy is the best player in MLS history and probably the best American player of all time. But he was left out of the US World Cup squad by coach **Jürgen Klinsmann**. Donovan missed the action in Brazil, but he put his name in the record books anyway. Early in the 2014 MLS season, he buried a shot against the Philadelphia Union. The goal was his 135th in MLS, making him the all-time scoring leader. He is also the all-time leading scorer in US Men's National Team history with 57 goals. In August, he announced that he was retiring from soccer.

Champions League

Other than the World Cup, the Champions League is the world's biggest soccer tournament. And they have it every year! Only the league champions and runners-up from Europe's top pro soccer leagues earn a spot in the long competition. Players are not representing their nations, but the clubs that pay their salaries. The Champions League (formerly called the European Cup) is a big deal to players and fans.

In 2014, Spanish fans had the most to cheer about. For the fifth time, two teams from the same country made the finals. They were even from the same city! Both Real Madrid and Atletico Madrid play in Spain's La Liga. Real was led by superstar Cristiano Ronaldo. Atletico was a bit of an upstart, and upset England's Chelsea to reach the final.

Atletico almost made it another upset, but Real scored in the final minutes to tie the game 1–1. In extra time, Real's deep lineup exploded for three goals—Gareth Bale's header was the first, then they added two more for a 4-1 final.

Gareth Bale starred in Champions League for Real Madrid.

Women's Soccer

The Seattle Reign dominated the 2014 National Women's Soccer League. Scottish star Kim Little led the league in goals, and the Reign lost only two games all season. But they couldn't nail down the championship. In a big upset, FC Kansas City knocked off the Reign, 2–1. KC's Amy Rodriguez scored two goals for the surprise champs!

Led by new coach Jill Ellis, the US women's national team played several friendlies in 2014, leading up to the CONCACAF championships in October. Those important games among North and Central American and Caribbean countries sent three finalists to the Women's World Cup, which will be played in 2015. That big event will be played in Canada, so the US should feel (mostly!) right at home.

10

That's not a very big number. But it's a big accomplishment. Real Madrid has won an all-time record Champions League or European Cup titles.

Stat Stuff

MAJOR LEAGUE SOCCER
CHAMPIONS

2013	Sporting Kansas City
2012	Los Angeles Galaxy
2011	Los Angeles Galaxy
2010	Colorado Rapids
2009	Real Salt Lake
2008	Columbus Crew
2007	Houston Dynamo
2006	Houston Dynamo
2005	Los Angeles Galaxy
2004	DC United
2003	San Jose Earthquakes
2002	Los Angeles Galaxy
2001	San Jose Earthquakes
2000	Kansas City Wizards
1999	DC United
1998	Chicago Fire
1997	DC United
1996	DC United

World Cup Scoring Leaders

MEN

GOALS	PLAYER, COUNTRY
16	Miroslav Klose, Germany
15	Ronaldo, Brazil
14	Gerd Müller, West Germany
13	Just Fontaine, France
12	Pelé, Brazil
11	Jürgen Klinsmann, Germany
11	Sandor Kocsis, Hungary

WOMEN

GOALS	PLAYER, COUNTRY
14	Birgit Prinz, Germany
14	Marta, Brazil
13	Abby Wambach, United States
12	Michelle Akers, United States

WOMEN'S WORLD CUP
ALL-TIME RESULTS

YEAR	CHAMPION	RUNNER-UP
2011	**Japan**	United States
2007	**Germany**	Brazil
2003	**Germany**	Sweden
1999	**United States**	China
1995	**Norway**	Germany
1991	**United States**	Norway

UEFA CHAMPIONS LEAGUE

The Champions League pits the best against the best. The top club teams from the members of UEFA (Union of European Football Associations) face off in a months-long tournament. They squeeze the games in among their regular league games, so the winners need to be talented and extremely fit. Read about the 2014 winner on page 73. Here are other recent Champions League champions!

2014 **Real Madrid**/SPAIN

2013 **Bayern Munich**/GERMANY

2012 **Chelsea FC**/ENGLAND

2011 **FC Barcelona**/SPAIN

2010 **Inter (Milan)**/ITALY

2009 **FC Barcelona**/SPAIN

2008 **Manchester United**/ENGLAND

2007 **AC Milan**/ITALY

2006 **FC Barcelona**/SPAIN

2005 **Liverpool FC**/ENGLAND

2004 **FC Porto**/PORTUGAL

2003 **AC Milan**/ITALY

2002 **Real Madrid**/SPAIN

2001 **Bayern Munich**/GERMANY

MLB

TIP OF THE CAP FOR CAP
Yankees shortstop and longtime captain Derek Jeter waved his thanks during the 2014 All-Star Game. In October, he played the final game of his career. He is surely headed for the Hall of Fame after 20 seasons in the bigs that included five World Series championships and more than 3,400 hits. Jeter's smooth, steady play anchored the Bronx Bombers since he was the 1996 A.L. Rookie of the Year.

Turnaround Time!

The 2013 Major League Baseball season was all about turnarounds. Teams that were struggling bounced back in record-setting ways. Teams that had not reached the playoffs in decades roared back. And the team that won it all came back from having its worst record since 1965.

The Los Angeles Dodgers were the biggest story of the summer of 2013. Packed with talent, they underperformed early on. But then a sparkplug from Cuba named **Yasiel Puig** showed up. Thanks to his hot start (seven homers and an all-time record 34 hits in his first 20 games) and the return of some injured stars, the Dodgers shocked baseball. From June 22 to August 17, their 42–8 record in a 50-game stretch was the best such streak since 1942.

Another NL team thrilled its longtime fans by returning to the playoffs. The Pittsburgh Pirates last played in the postseason in 1992, back when they had a guy named **Barry Bonds**.

ONE BIG OUT

One of the biggest stories of the 2013 season was the suspension of **Alex Rodriguez**. The Yankees' third baseman has 654 career homers and three MVP trophies. But Major League Baseball suspended him for using performance-enhancing drugs. He missed the second half of the 2013 season and will miss all of 2014. As great as A-Rod was, he broke the rules, and he'll pay the price.

Their new star was eventual NL MVP **Andrew McCutchen**. That all-around star led his team to a wild-card spot. Pirates manager **Clint Hurdle** said the team was inspired by legendary Pirate **Roberto Clemente**. That four-time batting champ wore No. 21 . . . and it would have been 21 years without the playoffs. So Hurdle said his team didn't want that to happen to Clemente's number!

The Boston Red Sox slumped in 2012, losing 93 games. But thanks to a very hairy group of players—and the league's best offense—the bearded bunch returned to the

Yasiel Puig arrived from Cuba to spark the Dodgers.

2013 FINAL STANDINGS

AL EAST

Red Sox	97–65
Rays	92–71
Orioles	85–77
Yankees	85–77
Blue Jays	74–88

AL CENTRAL

Tigers	93–69
Indians	92–70
Royals	86–76
Twins	66–96
White Sox	63–99

AL WEST

Athletics	96–66
Rangers	91–72
Angels	78–84
Mariners	71–91
Astros	51–111

NL EAST

Braves	96–66
Nationals	86–76
Mets	74–88
Phillies	73–89
Marlins	62–100

NL CENTRAL

Cardinals	97–65
Pirates	94–68
Reds	90–72
Brewers	74–88
Cubs	66–96

NL WEST

Dodgers	92–70
Diamondbacks	81–81
Padres	76–86
Giants	76–86
Rockies	74–88

McCutchen sparked a Pirates' rebound.

World Series for the third time since 2004.

The turnaround theme continued in September, the sport's most exciting month. The Texas Rangers looked like sure winners in the AL West. Then a 1–10 nosedive doomed their playoff hopes. Meanwhile, the scrappy Oakland Athletics went on an 11–2 run that helped them win the division, while Texas missed the postseason.

The AL wild-card spots went down to the final game, too. The Cleveland Indians finished the regular season on a 10–0 run to gain a surprise spot. The Tampa Bay Rays had to win eight of their final 10 games and then beat Texas in Game 163 to qualify for the playoffs.

The 2013 season saw the debut of an additional wild-card game. The two wild-card teams in each league played a one-game playoff to advance. The Indians' great run ended with a Rays shutout. In the NL, Pittsburgh continued its amazing season by beating the Reds.

The Playoffs!
DIVISION SERIES

Cardinals ace Adam Wainwright was lights out!

Cardinals 3, Pirates 2

The Pirates and their devoted fans were happy to be back in the playoffs for the first time in 20 years. They were not so happy to see the Cardinals win the final two games to clinch this series. St. Louis pitchers **Michael Wacha** and **Adam Wainwright** handcuffed Pittsburgh. Wainwright, who had tied for the NL lead with 19 wins, hurled a complete-game victory in Game 5 to clinch the series for St. Louis.

NATIONAL LEAGUE

Dodgers 3, Braves 1

Fans around the country got a good look at the Dodgers' Cuban sensation **Yasiel Puig**, who batted .471. His exciting play, backed by great pitching from Cy Young winner **Clayton Kershaw**, led LA to a win over Atlanta. The big blow came from third baseman **Juan Uribe**, who slugged a two-run homer late in Game 4 for a come-from-behind win.

BONUS ROUND

The MLB playoffs expanded for the first time since 1995. An additional wild-card team spot was given to each league. The two wild-card teams played off to earn the chance to advance to the Division Series. The results of the first Wild-Card Playoff:

AL Rays 4—Indians 0
Alex Cobb pitched a gem and Desmond Jennings had two big RBI.

NL Pirates 6—Reds 2
Russell Martin hit two homers as part of a 14-hit Pirates attack.

853

That's the mighty runs scored total put up by the bearded Boston Red Sox, the highest total in the Major Leagues in 2013.

Verlander clinched the series for Detroit.

AMERICAN LEAGUE

Red Sox 3, Rays 1

Power hitting by **David "Big Papi" Ortiz** and power pitching by **Jon Lester** and **John Lackey** led Boston to a win over Tampa Bay. Boston's season-long offensive power continued, as they scored 26 runs in four games. Tampa Bay had a bright light with a walk-off win in Game 3, but the Sox were too much in the end.

Tigers 3, Athletics 2

In the regular season, Tigers Cy Young Award winner **Max Scherzer** was the big story. In this series, Scherzer had two wins. Detroit's other ace, **Justin Verlander**, was dominant. He pitched 15 shutout innings and was the winning pitcher in Game 5, when he gave up only two hits in eight innings. The Tigers won the last two games of the series to return to the ALCS for the third straight year.

2013 Championship Series

ALCS

This series came down to the Red Sox hitters against the Tigers pitchers, but along the way fans had a blast watching some great baseball. In Game 1, Detroit nearly no-hit the Sox and held on for a dramatic 1–0 win. In Game 2, Boston was down to its last four outs. With the bases loaded and two outs in the eighth, **David "Big Papi" Ortiz** slugged a game-tying grand slam. It was the latest game-tying or winning grand slam in baseball playoff history. Fenway Park went wild! Boston scored again in the bottom of the ninth to win with a Tiger-stunning walk-off. Boston's **John Lackey** shut down Detroit to win Game 3, 1–0. After the Tigers tied

2,064

That's how many regular-season games **Carlos Beltran** played in 16 seasons before earning his first trip to a World Series.

the Series, Boston won the final two to earn a trip to the World Series. The big blow in Game 6 was a grand slam by **Shane Victorino**, who came into the at-bat 2-for-23 in the series!

NLCS

Would the Dodgers' miracle season continue in the postseason? A talented Cardinals team put a stop to that. Cardinals outfielder **Carlos Beltran** was the hero of Game 1, throwing out a run at home plate in extra innings before homering in the 13th to win it. In Game 2, Dodgers ace **Clayton Kershaw** did his job, limiting St. Louis to one run. The Cardinals pitchers were even better, though. Rookie **Michael Wacha** led a group that shut out the Dodgers and won 1–0. Back home in LA, the Dodgers and pitcher **Hyun-Jin Ryu** won Game 3. After the Cards won Game 4, LA stopped a late St. Louis rally to win Game 5. In Game 6, though, Wacha was awesome again. St. Louis earned its record 19th NL pennant with a 9–0 win.

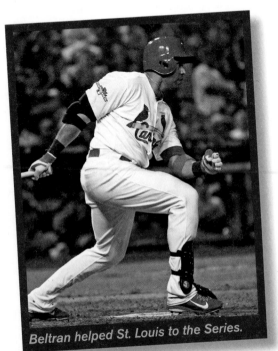

Beltran helped St. Louis to the Series.

2013 World Series

Worst to first: That's the turnaround story of the 2013 Boston Red Sox. The other story was the hideous beards many players grew. The hairiest, hard-hittingest team in baseball stormed through the season. In the World Series, they called on their leader, and Big Papi delivered. Along the way, fans saw some things no one had ever seen!

GAME 1: Red Sox 8–Cardinals 1

Three Cardinals errors opened the door, and the Sox strolled through. **Mike Napoli's** three-run double in the first was all that **Jon Lester** needed. He shut down the Cardinals for a pretty easy win.

GAME 2:
Cardinals 4–Red Sox 2

It was Boston's turn to give away runs. A pair of errors led to the go-ahead runs in the seventh. St. Louis rookie ace **Michael Wacha** did the rest.

GAME 3:
Cardinals 5–Red Sox 4

The World Series has been played since 1903, and never had a game ended like this one. With the score tied 4–4 in the bottom of the ninth, the Cardinals scored the winning run on a bizarre play. Trying to run from third, **Allen Craig** tripped over Boston's **Will Middlebrooks**, on the ground after making a diving try for the ball. Craig was thrown out at home, but the umps ruled that Middlebrooks had "obstructed" Craig, or gotten in his way. According to the rules, the umps awarded St. Louis the winning run!

GAME 4:
Red Sox 4–Cardinals 2

After **Big Papi** called a huddle to rally his team, **Jonny Gomes** answered with a three-run homer. The clutch sixth-inning shot helped Boston even the Series.

GAME 5: Red Sox 3–Cardinals 1

Big stars shine on the biggest stages. Red Sox ace **Jon Lester** won his second game of the Series, allowing four hits and one run in 7 2/3 innings. **Big Papi** had three more hits to raise his Series average to .733.

GAME 6: Red Sox 6–Cardinals 1

St. Louis finally wised up and walked **Big Papi** four times. But **Stephen Drew** homered to lead a six-run Boston attack. **John Lackey** pitched a gem, and Boston clinched its third world championship since 2004, the most by any team in baseball in the 2000s!

Ace closer Koji Uehara exults!

95

Years it had been since the Red Sox won a World Series in Fenway Park, their home since 1912.

Award Winners

MOST VALUABLE PLAYER
AL: **MIGUEL CABRERA**, TIGERS
NL: **ANDREW McCUTCHEN**, PIRATES

CY YOUNG AWARD
AL: **MAX SCHERZER**, TIGERS
NL: **CLAYTON KERSHAW**, DODGERS

ROOKIE OF THE YEAR
AL: **WIL MYERS**, RAYS
NL: **JOSE FERNANDEZ**, MARLINS

MANAGER OF THE YEAR
AL: **TERRY FRANCONA**, INDIANS
NL: **CLINT HURDLE**, PIRATES

HANK AARON AWARD
AL: **MIGUEL CABRERA**, TIGERS
NL: **PAUL GOLDSCHMIDT**, DIAMONDBACKS

ROBERTO CLEMENTE AWARD
(for community service)
CARLOS BELTRAN, CARDINALS

Clayton Kershaw won his second Cy Young Award in three seasons.

Stat Champs

AL Hitting Leaders

53 HOME RUNS
138 RBI
Chris Davis, Orioles

.348 BATTING AVERAGE
Miguel Cabrera, Tigers ▶▶▶

52 STOLEN BASES
Jacoby Ellsbury, Red Sox

199 HITS
Adrian Beltre, Rangers

NL Hitting Leaders

.331 BATTING AVERAGE
Michael Cuddyer, Rockies

36 HOME RUNS
Pedro Alvarez, Pirates
Paul Goldschmidt,
Diamondbacks

125 RBI
Paul Goldschmidt, Diamondbacks

46 STOLEN BASES
Eric Young, Rockies and Mets

AL Pitching Leaders

21 WINS
Max Scherzer, Tigers

50 SAVES
Jim Johnson, Orioles

2.57 ERA
Anibal Sanchez, Tigers

277 STRIKEOUTS
Yu Darvish, Rangers

NL Pitching Leaders

19 WINS
Adam Wainwright, Cardinals
Jordan Zimmerman, Nationals

50 SAVES
Craig Kimbrel, Braves

1.83 ERA
232 STRIKEOUTS
Clayton Kershaw, Dodgers

2013 Highlights

Some of the best stories of individual success from 2013:

✳ Baltimore first baseman **Chris Davis** (right) was the year's top slugger. He set a new Orioles single-season record with 53 homers. He also led the AL in homers and RBI, preventing **Miguel Cabrera** from earning back-to-back Triple Crowns.

✳ Watch for more from "Sliding" **Billy Hamilton** in 2014. The super-speedster had an amazing big-league debut in 2013. He became the first player since 1920 to steal four bases in his first game! The Reds' outfielder was brought up to help Cincy chase a playoff spot. He actually led the team in steals even though he played for less than two months!

◀◀◀✳ On August 23, Yankees outfielder **Ichiro Suzuki** became the third player ever to reach 4,000 career hits. There's an asterisk, however: He got the first 1,277 while playing in the Japanese pro league. Still, he's in good company. The other two 4,000-hit men? **Ty Cobb** and **Pete Rose**.

✳ Detroit pitcher **Max Scherzer** started the season 19–1, the first pitcher to do so since 1912.

✳ Fans got their money's worth in 2013. Teams combined to play 239 extra-inning games, the most ever.

✳ The amazing Angels outfielder **Mike Trout** continued his amazingness: He became the youngest player ever with two straight seasons of 20 homers and 30 steals.

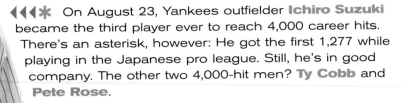
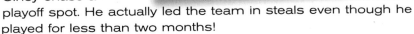

Wild and Wacky!

A look at some of the goofier events and feats from 2013.

➜ After chasing a foul ball along the first-base line and watching it bounce into the seats, Tigers first baseman **Prince Fielder** grabbed a chip from a fan's nacho plate!

"It was amazing. This dude just comes out of the stands and says, 'It's okay. I'm a beekeeper."

— ANGELS PITCHER **C.J. WILSON** ABOUT THE MAN WHO SAVED THE DAY FOR THE BEE-BUZZED BASEBALL GAME

➜ In September, a game between the Angels and Mariners was delayed twice by swarms of bees on the field!

➜ Rays pitcher **Alex Cobb** did something no one had ever done: He struck out four guys in one inning and gave up a run. Huh? After his first K, the batter reached on a wild pitch. The batter then stole second and third and scored on another wild pitch!

➜ On June 5, the Mariners and White Sox played 13 innings of scoreless baseball. Then they EACH scored 5 runs in the 14th! Chicago won with two more runs in the 16th.

1,535

This is not a big number anyone wants. The Astros set an all-time single-season record by striking out that many times in 2013. But hey, they're still in the big leagues!

NEARLY PERFECT

Three pitchers came within an eyelash of perfect games in 2013. **Yu Darvish** of Texas (right) gave up a two-out single to Houston's **Marwin Gonzalez**. Detroit's **Anibal Sanchez** walked the first batter of the game, but then gave up no hits until the bottom of the ninth; **Joe Mauer** of Minnesota spoiled the no-no. Finally, the Giants' **Yusmeiro Petit** missed a perfecto by one out, as Arizona's **Eric Chavez** singled.

On the final day of the regular season, another first for fans: Miami's **Henderson Alvarez** won a no-hitter when the Tigers let in the winning run on a wild pitch. It was the first wild-pitch, walk-off no-hitter ever!

Quick Hits: 2014

Best Game Ever Pitched? ▶▶▶

On June 18, the Dodgers' amazing **Clayton Kershaw** did something no other pitcher has ever done. He no-hit the Colorado Rockies while striking out fifteen and allowing no walks. That was the most Ks ever in a no-no with no BBs. According to some experts, it was the best game ever pitched. Another measurement put it second-best (behind **Kerry Wood's** 20-strikeout, one-hit performance in 1998). The only baserunner was **Corey Dickerson**, who reached on an error by shortstop **Hanley Ramirez**. The no-hitter was Kershaw's first (to go along with two Cy Young Awards), and was part of a 41-inning scoreless streak.

Umps Watching TV

Video replay has been used in the major leagues for several years. Umpires could look at a video replay at the ballpark to decide if a ball was a homer, for instance. But it could only be used for a small number of plays. That changed in 2014. Now, managers can make challenges of umpires' calls (except for balls and strikes). Officials at the league office in New York then look at the replays. Then they let the umps on the field know if the call was right or wrong.

After some early glitches, the system seemed to be working well. Some calls were overturned, others were pronounced "good."

One thing the new system reduced: managers spending lots of time kicking dirt, screaming their heads off, and throwing things! However, the system also means that they can only argue about balls and strikes . . . and they did, with ejections by umps actually going up in the first half of the season, according to *USA Today*.

The Captain Waves Good-bye

In 2013, the Yankees and baseball said good-bye to closer **Mariano Rivera**. In 2014, it was shortstop **Derek Jeter**'s time to say farewell. The Yankees' longtime captain called it a career after 20 seasons in pinstripes. He left behind an amazing legacy, including enough hits to rank seventh all-time, a .417 batting average in All-Star Games, and five World Series championships (he hit .321 in his seven Fall Classics). He won five Gold Gloves and was named to 14 All-Star Games, while also winning the 2000 World Series MVP. Jeter was one of baseball's classiest players, never flashy, just steady and outstanding. He leaves a big hole in the Yankees infield.

Amazing Feats!

* Dodgers pitcher **Zach Grienke** wound up a streak of 21 straight games allowing two or fewer runs while pitching at least five, a streak not accomplished for more than a century!

* **Jose Abreu** was named the AL Player and Rookie of the Month for April. The White Sox first baseman from Cuba had 10 home runs in the month. That broke a rookie record set by **Albert Pujols** back in 2001.

* **Pujols** has done pretty well since setting that record. In fact, in 2014, he reached a big milestone. On April 22, he hit his 499th and 500th career homers.

* Red Sox DH **David Ortiz** and White Sox first baseman **Adam Dunn** each hit their 450th career homers.

* Indians third baseman **Lonnie Chisenhall** had a pretty good day on June 9. He had three homers among his five hits, and had nine RBI. He was the first since 1975 to do that and only the fourth ever.

* Giants pitcher **Tim Lincecum** must really like pitching against the Padres. On June 25, he threw a no-hitter against them. Nothing new, though. In 2013, he also no-hit the Padres. He was the first pitcher to throw two no-nos at the same team since Hall of Famer **Addie Joss** way back in 1910.

Pujols slammed a pair to reach 500.

World Series Winners

YEAR	WINNER	RUNNER-UP	SCORE*	YEAR	WINNER	RUNNER-UP	SCORE*
2013	Boston Red Sox	St. Louis Cardinals	4-2	1986	New York Mets	Boston Red Sox	4-3
2012	San Francisco Giants	Detroit Tigers	4-0	1985	Kansas City Royals	St. Louis Cardinals	4-3
2011	St. Louis Cardinals	Texas Rangers	4-3	1984	Detroit Tigers	San Diego Padres	4-1
2010	San Francisco Giants	Texas Rangers	4-1	1983	Baltimore Orioles	Philadelphia Phillies	4-1
2009	New York Yankees	Philadelphia Phillies	4-2	1982	St. Louis Cardinals	Milwaukee Brewers	4-3
2008	Philadelphia Phillies	Tampa Bay Rays	4-1	1981	Los Angeles Dodgers	New York Yankees	4-2
2007	Boston Red Sox	Colorado Rockies	4-0	1980	Philadelphia Phillies	Kansas City Royals	4-2
2006	St. Louis Cardinals	Detroit Tigers	4-1	1979	Pittsburgh Pirates	Baltimore Orioles	4-3
2005	Chicago White Sox	Houston Astros	4-0	1978	New York Yankees	Los Angeles Dodgers	4-2
2004	Boston Red Sox	St. Louis Cardinals	4-0	1977	New York Yankees	Los Angeles Dodgers	4-2
2003	Florida Marlins	New York Yankees	4-2	1976	Cincinnati Reds	New York Yankees	4-0
2002	Anaheim Angels	San Francisco Giants	4-3	1975	Cincinnati Reds	Boston Red Sox	4-3
2001	Arizona Diamondbacks	New York Yankees	4-3	1974	Oakland Athletics	Los Angeles Dodgers	4-1
2000	New York Yankees	New York Mets	4-1	1973	Oakland Athletics	New York Mets	4-3
1999	New York Yankees	Atlanta Braves	4-0	1972	Oakland Athletics	Cincinnati Reds	4-3
1998	New York Yankees	San Diego Padres	4-0	1971	Pittsburgh Pirates	Baltimore Orioles	4-3
1997	Florida Marlins	Cleveland Indians	4-3	1970	Baltimore Orioles	Cincinnati Reds	4-1
1996	New York Yankees	Atlanta Braves	4-2	1969	New York Mets	Baltimore Orioles	4-1
1995	Atlanta Braves	Cleveland Indians	4-2	1968	Detroit Tigers	St. Louis Cardinals	4-3
1993	Toronto Blue Jays	Philadelphia Phillies	4-2	1967	St. Louis Cardinals	Boston Red Sox	4-3
1992	Toronto Blue Jays	Atlanta Braves	4-2	1966	Baltimore Orioles	Los Angeles Dodgers	4-0
1991	Minnesota Twins	Atlanta Braves	4-3	1965	Los Angeles Dodgers	Minnesota Twins	4-3
1990	Cincinnati Reds	Oakland Athletics	4-0	1964	St. Louis Cardinals	New York Yankees	4-3
1989	Oakland Athletics	San Francisco Giants	4-0	1963	Los Angeles Dodgers	New York Yankees	4-0
1988	Los Angeles Dodgers	Oakland Athletics	4-1	1962	New York Yankees	San Francisco Giants	4-3
1987	Minnesota Twins	St. Louis Cardinals	4-3	1961	New York Yankees	Cincinnati Reds	4-1

* Score is represented in games played.

YEAR	WINNER	RUNNER-UP	SCORE*	YEAR	WINNER	RUNNER-UP	SCORE*
1960	Pittsburgh Pirates	New York Yankees	4-3	1931	St. Louis Cardinals	Philadelphia Athletics	4-3
1959	Los Angeles Dodgers	Chicago White Sox	4-2	1930	Philadelphia Athletics	St. Louis Cardinals	4-2
1958	New York Yankees	Milwaukee Braves	4-3	1929	Philadelphia Athletics	Chicago Cubs	4-1
1957	Milwaukee Braves	New York Yankees	4-3	1928	New York Yankees	St. Louis Cardinals	4-0
1956	New York Yankees	Brooklyn Dodgers	4-3	1927	New York Yankees	Pittsburgh Pirates	4-0
1955	Brooklyn Dodgers	New York Yankees	4-3	1926	St. Louis Cardinals	New York Yankees	4-3
1954	New York Giants	Cleveland Indians	4-0	1925	Pittsburgh Pirates	Washington Senators	4-3
1953	New York Yankees	Brooklyn Dodgers	4-2	1924	Washington Senators	New York Giants	4-3
1952	New York Yankees	Brooklyn Dodgers	4-3	1923	New York Yankees	New York Giants	4-2
1951	New York Yankees	New York Giants	4-2	1922	New York Giants	New York Yankees	4-0
1950	New York Yankees	Philadelphia Phillies	4-0	1921	New York Giants	New York Yankees	5-3
1949	New York Yankees	Brooklyn Dodgers	4-1	1920	Cleveland Indians	Brooklyn Dodgers	5-2
1948	Cleveland Indians	Boston Braves	4-2	1919	Cincinnati Reds	Chicago White Sox	5-3
1947	New York Yankees	Brooklyn Dodgers	4-3	1918	Boston Red Sox	Chicago Cubs	4-2
1946	St. Louis Cardinals	Boston Red Sox	4-3	1917	Chicago White Sox	New York Giants	4-2
1945	Detroit Tigers	Chicago Cubs	4-3	1916	Boston Red Sox	Brooklyn Dodgers	4-1
1944	St. Louis Cardinals	St. Louis Browns	4-2	1915	Boston Red Sox	Philadelphia Phillies	4-1
1943	New York Yankees	St. Louis Cardinals	4-1	1914	Boston Braves	Philadelphia Athletics	4-0
1942	St. Louis Cardinals	New York Yankees	4-1	1913	Philadelphia Athletics	New York Giants	4-1
1941	New York Yankees	Brooklyn Dodgers	4-1	1912	Boston Red Sox	New York Giants	4-3
1940	Cincinnati Reds	Detroit Tigers	4-3	1911	Philadelphia Athletics	New York Giants	4-2
1939	New York Yankees	Cincinnati Reds	4-0	1910	Philadelphia Athletics	Chicago Cubs	4-1
1938	New York Yankees	Chicago Cubs	4-0	1909	Pittsburgh Pirates	Detroit Tigers	4-3
1937	New York Yankees	New York Giants	4-1	1908	Chicago Cubs	Detroit Tigers	4-1
1936	New York Yankees	New York Giants	4-2	1907	Chicago Cubs	Detroit Tigers	4-0
1935	Detroit Tigers	Chicago Cubs	4-2	1906	Chicago White Sox	Chicago Cubs	4-2
1934	St. Louis Cardinals	Detroit Tigers	4-3	1905	New York Giants	Philadelphia Athletics	4-1
1933	New York Giants	Washington Senators	4-1	1903	Boston Red Sox	Pittsburgh Pirates	5-3
1932	New York Yankees	Chicago Cubs	4-0				

Note: 1904 not played because NL-champion Giants refused to play; 1994 not played due to MLB work stoppage.

COLLEGE BASKETBALL

TO THE HOOP!
Connecticut's Shabazz Napier got the bucket on this play. His team got the brass ring, too, winning the NCAA National Championship over Kentucky to wrap up an exciting Final Four.

Men's Basketball

College basketball experts love to predict. They pick preseason Top 10s and All-Americans. They tell you in October who is going to win in April. For the 2013–14 season, they must have been looking at some pretty cloudy crystal balls! The team that won it all, Connecticut, started out ranked in the 20s in most polls. A team that played in one of the less-famous conferences streaked through the season without a loss. Wichita State was 34–0 in the season to earn one of the four No. 1 seeds in the NCAA tournament (page 98). The Orangemen of Syracuse nearly matched that run. They won 25 straight before falling to Boston College in February. The Big Ten had three teams (Michigan, Wisconsin, and Michigan State) that each won at least 28 games.

Meanwhile, some of the top teams expected to rise to the top fell by the wayside, including Duke, Oregon, and

Arizona reached the top of the polls in December, but was one of many to fall from No. 1.

FINAL MEN'S TOP 10
USA Today Coaches Poll

1. Connecticut
2. Kentucky
3. Florida
4. Wisconsin
5. Arizona
6. Michigan
7. Wichita State
8. Michigan State
9. Louisville
10. Virginia

The end-of-season conference tournaments had some surprises of their own. Perhaps the biggest came when Cal Poly San Luis Obispo won the Big West Conference tournament. Cal Poly had been only 14–20 in the regular season.

In the end, 68 teams made it to the "Big Dance." Once they were there, they put on one of the best shows of high-quality basketball in many years. Any one of a dozen teams showed the skills and teamwork to win it, but when the dribbling stopped, only one team was on top of the heap. Say hello to the national champion Connecticut Huskies!

Oklahoma State. Former "Cinderellas," including Butler and Gonzaga, found that the magic was tapped out.

The season started with a fantastic opener, as four former championship schools met in a super doubleheader in November. Michigan State beat Kentucky, while Kansas knocked Duke to set the early pace in the race to the top (see page 96). Michigan State didn't stay on top long, however, and by December, Arizona was installed as the No. 1 team.

That started a season-long revolving door at the top. Though Arizona held on for two months, that was the longest run by any of the schools that ranked first. Kentucky, Syracuse, and Florida each also had several weeks on top before losing key games . . . and their No. 1 ranking.

As the season wound down, the college hoops world watched a guy nicknamed "Dougie McBuckets" with joy (except if you were playing him). **Doug McDermott** of Creighton poured in points like syrup on pancakes, nailing threes and making tough jumpers. He ended up carrying home most of the player-of-the-year awards (page 97).

Michigan State soared early in the season.

Hoop Highlights

Top Two

For the first time since 2008, the No. 1 and No. 2 teams met in the regular season. Okay, it was just about the start of the year for both teams, but still, it was a great tip-off for the season. No. 1 Kentucky boasted a group of amazing freshman players. No. 2 Michigan State had high hopes, after just missing the Final Four a year earlier. They met in the Champions Classic, and their matchup was a classic indeed. A tip-in by the Spartans' **Branden Dawson** cemented the MSU win, 78–74.

Early Upset

North Carolina is one of the most successful college basketball schools. They're annually among the top teams, but that makes them a target. In November, in only their fourth game of the year, the Belmont Bruins shocked No. 12-ranked UNC.

With great three-point shooting and clutch free throws, Belmont beat the Tar Heels, 83–80. **J. J. Mann** had the last of Belmont's "treys" to seal the win. Pretty good way to start the season!

Mr. Clutch

Syracuse had one of the best runs of success of any team during the season. But they almost ended their run a game early if not for the heroics of freshman guard **Tyler Ennis**. With 4.4 seconds left, and his team trailing by a point, Ennis powered across midcourt with the ball. From 35 feet, he buried a buzzer-beating, three-point shot that gave the Orangemen a come-from-behind win over Pittsburgh.

◄◄◄ McBuckets!

Doug McDermott of Creighton does not get the headlines for dunks or amazing leaping ability. What he does is just pour in points . . . in

WHAT A BEGINNING

Duke and Syracuse are two of the most famous basketball schools in the country. Duke coach **Mike Krzyzewski** has more wins than any Division 1 coach . . . Syracuse's **Jim Boeheim** is second! Yet these two teams had only met twice before connecting in Syracuse in February. But it was worth the wait, as they collided for what most called the best game of the season, a thrilling 91–89 Syracuse win in overtime. "That was one of the best games I've ever seen," said Boeheim. The intense back-and-forth action came down to a long three-point shot by Duke's **Rasheed Sulaimon** that beat the buzzer and sent the game to OT. Foul trouble by Duke led to clutch free-throw shooting by Syracuse that sealed the win. Look for more great games in the future: This was Syracuse's first season in the ACC, so they'll play twice a year from now on.

buckets! Nicknamed "Dougie McBuckets," the Bluejay's scoring skills helped him earn the Wooden and Naismith Awards as the nation's top player in 2014. He led the NCAA in scoring (26.7 ppg) for the second consecutive year. His 3,150 career points are the fifth-most all-time and the highest total in more than two decades.

504

Oakland University's **Travis Bader** poured in that many three-point baskets in his career, setting a new all-time NCAA record!

March Madness!

The Flyers' upset string had the basketball world buzzing.

▶ The First No. 2 seed to fall was Villanova, which went ice-cold shooting against eventual champ Connecticut, a No. 7 seed.

▶ Wichita State waved good-bye to its perfect season thanks to No. 8-seed Kentucky's upset in the second round. Led by five freshmen, the Wildcats shocked the Shockers, who were the first No. 1 seed to fall.

▶ Stanford had had an up-and-down season, but then had a big pair of ups in March. Seeded No. 10, they first beat No. 7 New Mexico, then amazed fans with a big win over No. 2 Kansas!

▶ Gotta love the drama: In the second round, five games went into overtime, more than twice as many as the past two tournaments put together.

▶ Dayton Flies! The biggest story of the early rounds was the play of the Dayton Flyers. Seeded No. 11, they first surprised a solid Ohio State team in the opening round. Then they topped that by beating No. 3 Syracuse, which had had a 25–0 run earlier in the year. In a battle of upset-makers, Dayton beat No. 10 Stanford to reach the Elite Eight. That's where the Flyers finally fell to earth, losing to No. 1 Florida.

Talk about lack of respect: One pre-tournament poll had Connecticut at No. 23 out of the 68-team field. Oops. The Huskies put on a tremendous run to the Final Four and then powered past two great teams to win the school's fourth national championship and first since 2011. Here are some of the tournament highlights:

▶ Duke's Blue Devils were blue after a first-round upset loss to No. 14-seed Mercer. The loss capped off a disappointing season for Duke, which always expects at least a spot in the Sweet 16.

▶ Brains over Bears: Harvard, the only Ivy League team in the tournament, knocked off No. 5-seed Cincinnati. It was nothing new for the Crimson, which beat a No. 3 seed in 2013!

▶ The only Regional Championship game between a No. 1 (Arizona) and a No. 2 (Wisconsin) went to overtime. The Badgers pulled out a 64–63 squeaker to make it to the Final Four.

▶ Kentucky's **Aaron Harrison** put his team into the Final Four with a three-point basket with 2.6 seconds left. The bucket gave the Wildcats a win over No. 2 Michigan, 75–72.

FINAL FOUR!

GAME 1: Florida had been one of the power teams of the season, using a strong frontcourt and veteran guards to earn a No. 1 seed. They were a high-scoring team, but in this game, they ran into a defense they couldn't solve. Connecticut shut down Florida and won 63–53.

GAME 2: The **Harrison brothers** gave the Kentucky Wildcats a spot in the championship game. **Andrew H.** passed to **Aaron H.**, who buried a three-point shot with 5.7 seconds left. That put the Wildcats ahead of the Wisconsin Badgers to stay, 74–73. Wisconsin missed only one free throw all game, a Final Four record, but it proved to be a big one.

NATIONAL CHAMPIONSHIP GAME:

For the first time ever, a No. 7 seed would play a No. 8 seed for the national title. It was also the first time since the tournament started using seeds that the final was played without a No. 1, 2, or 3 in the game! The matchup said a lot about how even college basketball had become. There are no more dominant teams, just gritty ones that battle through the brackets. In fact, Connecticut was ranked No. 26 overall by the selection committee; Kentucky was just below them at 29.

Connecticut was led by a solid senior, guard **Shabazz Napier**. Kentucky relied on a group of freshmen. In the end, experience beat the rookies. Napier had 22 points, along with 14 from **Ryan Boatright**. Connecticut had actually been banned from the 2013 tournament after breaking some NCAA rules, so the title was even sweeter. In his second season after taking over from legendary coach **Jim Calhoun**, UConn coach **Kevin Ollie** helped his team cut the nets after a well-deserved 60–54 win.

Women's Basketball

Talk about a dominating performance: The University of Connecticut women powered through the season undefeated to capture their ninth national championship. The Huskies defeated every opponent by at least 10 points, including eight games in which they were on top by 50 points or more. Now that's dominating!

Travel Team

In December, the Connecticut Huskies traveled to play Duke in a game most expected to be tight. It wasn't. UConn won 83–61 and gave the rest of the schools early notice that this would be their year. Superstar **Breanna Stewart** had 24 points for the Huskies. Then in January, UConn did it again, knocking off a top rival while on the road. Baylor had not lost on its home court since 2010, but the Huskies ended that streak with a 66–55 win in January.

FINAL WOMEN'S TOP 10
USA Today Coaches Poll

1. Connecticut
2. Notre Dame
3. Stanford
4. Maryland
5. Louisville
6. Baylor
7. North Carolina
8. Tennessee
9. South Carolina
10. Texas A&M

◀◀◀ OT OT OT OT

Kentucky and Baylor were having so much fun in their game in December, they just kept playing. The teams combined for an all-time NCAA record 263 points and needed four overtimes to determine a winner. A layup very late in overtime No. 4 by Kentucky's **Jennifer O'Neill** helped the Wildcats finally claim victory. Baylor had to play the final three OTs without leading scorer **Odyssey Sims**, who had fouled out after scoring a career-high 47 points.

Stewart stomped the Irish.

FINAL FOUR

Unlike the men's tournament, the women's tournament featured few upsets in the early rounds. No. 12 BYU was the only high seed to make any noise. In the first round, they beat No. 5 North Carolina State handily. In the next round, No. 4 Nebraska fell to BYU. Their reward for the upsets? A game against undefeated Connecticut. Oh, well. No. 7 DePaul had the other big upset, defeating No. 2-ranked Duke. Otherwise, every regional final included teams seeded 1 through 4.

In the Final Four, UConn easily beat Stanford and its All-America star **Chiney Ogwumike**. Notre Dame continued its own undefeated run by knocking off Maryland. The Terrapins had reached this game by defeating No. 1-seed Tennessee, which continued its amazing success. The school has been part of all 33 NCAA women's tournaments ever played.

Championship Game

For the first time, a pair of undefeated teams met for the national title. UConn had been here before, of course. They had four previous undefeated seasons. But Notre Dame had won all its games to this point for the first time in school history. Only one of these two great schools would end the game undefeated, however.

The result was clear early. The UConn defense was just too much, even for Notre Dame's talented scorers. In fact, the 58 points by the Fighting Irish were a season low. On offense, N.D. had no answer for All-American **Breanna Stewart**, who scored a team-high 21 points.

Western Surprise

Stanford was ranked No. 3 and figured on another easy win over unranked Washington. But the Huskies had other ideas and stunned the Cardinal in February. Stanford was ice-cold from outside, making just 21 percent of their three-point attempts. It was the first conference road loss for Stanford in 62 games, and a rare victory for an unranked team against a top-10 opponent.

Player of the Year

It was no surprise that the team of the year had the player of the year. Connecticut sophomore **Breanna Stewart** won the Naismith Award as well as the player of the year award from the Associated Press. Stewart is the sixth player from the amazing UConn program to win the Naismith. Baylor senior **Odyssey Sims** won the Wade Award, given by the Women's Basketball Coaches Association.

NCAA Champs!

MEN'S DIVISION I

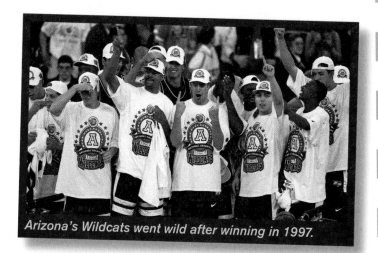

Arizona's Wildcats went wild after winning in 1997.

		1992 **Duke**
		1991 **Duke**
		1990 **UNLV**
		1989 **Michigan**
		1988 **Kansas**
		1987 **Indiana**
		1986 **Louisville**
		1985 **Villanova**
		1984 **Georgetown**
		1983 **NC State**
2014 **Connecticut**	2003 **Syracuse**	1982 **North Carolina**
2013 **Louisville**	2002 **Maryland**	1981 **Indiana**
2012 **Kentucky**	2001 **Duke**	1980 **Louisville**
2011 **Connecticut**	2000 **Michigan State**	1979 **Michigan State**
2010 **Duke**	1999 **Connecticut**	1978 **Kentucky**
2009 **North Carolina**	1998 **Kentucky**	1977 **Marquette**
2008 **Kansas**	1997 **Arizona**	1976 **Indiana**
2007 **Florida**	1996 **Kentucky**	1975 **UCLA**
2006 **Florida**	1995 **UCLA**	1974 **NC State**
2005 **North Carolina**	1994 **Arkansas**	1973 **UCLA**
2004 **Connecticut**	1993 **North Carolina**	1972 **UCLA**

1971 **UCLA**	1947 **Holy Cross**	1942 **Stanford**
1970 **UCLA**	1946 **Oklahoma A&M**	1941 **Wisconsin**
1969 **UCLA**	1945 **Oklahoma A&M**	1940 **Indiana**
1968 **UCLA**	1944 **Utah**	1939 **Oregon**
1967 **UCLA**	1943 **Wyoming**	
1966 **Texas Western**		
1965 **UCLA**		

WOMEN'S DIVISION I

1964 **UCLA**	2014 **Connecticut**	1997 **Tennessee**
1963 **Loyola (Illinois)**	2013 **Connecticut**	1996 **Tennessee**
1962 **Cincinnati**	2012 **Baylor**	1995 **Connecticut**
1961 **Cincinnati**	2011 **Texas A&M**	1994 **North Carolina**
1960 **Ohio State**	2010 **Connecticut**	1993 **Texas Tech**
1959 **California**	2009 **Connecticut**	1992 **Stanford**
1958 **Kentucky**	2008 **Tennessee**	1991 **Tennessee**
1957 **North Carolina**	2007 **Tennessee**	1990 **Stanford**
1956 **San Francisco**	2006 **Maryland**	1989 **Tennessee**
1955 **San Francisco**	2005 **Baylor**	1988 **Louisiana Tech**
1954 **La Salle**	2004 **Connecticut**	1987 **Tennessee**
1953 **Indiana**	2003 **Connecticut**	1986 **Texas**
1952 **Kansas**	2002 **Connecticut**	1985 **Old Dominion**
1951 **Kentucky**	2001 **Notre Dame**	1984 **USC**
1950 **City Coll. of N.Y.**	2000 **Connecticut**	1983 **USC**
1949 **Kentucky**	1999 **Purdue**	1982 **Louisiana Tech**
1948 **Kentucky**	1998 **Tennessee**	

NBA

PAINT IN THE PAINT

Miami's Chris Andersen shows off some impressive tattoos, but San Antonio's Kawhi Leonard painted a better picture. The young forward was named the NBA Finals MVP as his Spurs knocked off the two-time defending champion Heat.

NBA 2013-14

Like a bouncing basketball, NBA teams went up and teams went down. But in the end, the same four teams were in the conference finals as last seaon. For the Miami Heat, there was no three-peat, however. The San Antonio Spurs' veteran core led them to their fifth NBA championship.

Moving across the nation, here's a look at some of the highlights of the season that led up to that championship series.

Toronto was a surprise winner of the Eastern Division. They were led to 48 wins by **DeMar DeRozan**'s All-Star season.

The Knicks added a new sort of star. In March, the team hired **Phil Jackson** to be the team president. Jackson won 11 NBA titles as the coach of the Bulls and Lakers. He brought in **Derek Fisher**, who played for Phil on the Lakers championship teams, to coach.

Another East Coast surprise was the Charlotte Bobcats. Led by star **Al Jefferson**, they improved their league-worst defense dramatically in 2013-14. Their winning record was their first since 2010.

In the Midwest, the Chicago Bulls had the best record in the Eastern Conference from January 1 to the end of the season, and newly signed forward **Pau Gasol** gives star guard **Derrick Rose** a big target.

Thanks to the big news in Cleveland (see page 107), the Cavaliers should be a new beast in the East in 2014-15.

The New Orleans Pelicans didn't fly very high, but young star **Anthony Davis** did. He led the NBA in blocks per game and looks to be on the verge of superstardom.

On the West Coast, the two Los Angeles teams continued their opposite paths. The once-mighty Lakers had one of their worst seasons ever, winning only 27 games, their fewest since 1960! Plus they watched former star **Dwight Howard** soar for the Houston Rockets. The Clippers, meanwhile, behind the power of **Blake Griffin** and the creativity of **Chris Paul**, won the Pacific Division for the second straight year.

The Phoenix Suns had the biggest year-to-year rise. They won 23 more games than 2013-14.

Can any of these teams on the rise overcome the Heat and Spurs? Offseason team moves will play a big part, especially those "welcome home" signs in Cleveland!

Dwight Howard

2013–14 FINAL STANDINGS

EASTERN CONFERENCE

ATLANTIC DIVISION

	W–L
Raptors	48–34
Nets	44–38
Knicks	37–45
Celtics	25–57
76ers	19–63

CENTRAL DIVISION

	W–L
Pacers	56–26
Bulls	48–34
Cavaliers	33–49
Pistons	29–53
Bucks	15–67

SOUTHEAST DIVISION

	W–L
Heat	54–28
Wizards	44–38
Bobcats	43–39
Hawks	38–44
Magic	23–59

WESTERN CONFERENCE

NORTHWEST DIVISION

	W–L
Thunder	59–23
Trail Blazers	54–28
Timberwolves	40–42
Nuggets	36–46
Jazz	25–57

PACIFIC DIVISION

	W–L
Clippers	57–25
Warriors	51–31
Suns	48–34
Kings	28–54
Lakers	27–55

SOUTHWEST DIVISION

	W–L
Spurs	62–20
Rockets	54–28
Grizzlies	50–32
Mavericks	49–33
Pelicans	34–48

RETURN OF
THE KING!

The biggest news of 2014–15 NBA season happened before a single shot was taken. In July, free agent **LeBron James** announced that he was leaving the Miami Heat to sign with Cleveland Cavaliers, his hometown team. He grew up there, and then was with the Cavs from 2003–2010. Cleveland fans rejoiced; Heat fans . . . did not. Cleveland later announced the signing of three-time All-Star power forward **Kevin Love**. Along with the Cavs' current players, the addition of these two superstars will make Cleveland an NBA title hopeful.

2014 NBA Playoffs

FIRST ROUND HIGHLIGHTS

Some experts called this the best first round ever. Five of the eight first-round series needed all seven games to find the winners.

➤ Portland's **LaMarcus Aldridge** scored 46 points and pulled down 18 rebounds in Game 1 as Portland beat Houston.

➤ The Wizards surprised the Bulls. Washington moved to the second round for the first time since 2005.

➤ The Clippers survived a scare from a gritty Warriors team led by sharpshooter **Stephen Curry**.

➤ No. 1 West seed San Antonio was pushed to the limit by the Mavericks. But the Spurs routed Dallas in Game 7, 119–96. In the East, the Pacers needed seven games to defeat the pesky Hawks.

➤ The best of this series of bests was probably the Thunder–Grizzlies matchup.

Four consecutives games went to overtime. Oklahoma City, led by **Kevin Durant**, had all it could handle from Memphis, but in the end, the Thunder made the most noise.

SEMIFINALS

➤ The Clippers might have been distracted by their owner's mistakes (see page 112). It didn't help that **Blake Griffin** and company could not stop **Kevin Durant** and **Russell Westbrook**.

➤ San Antonio sent Portland home in five games.

➤ Miami lost its first game of the playoffs, but Brooklyn's dream season ended in five games.

➤ Indiana did not look like the dominant team they had been in the regular season, but **Paul George** and his teammates had enough to defeat the Wizards.

CONFERENCE FINALS

➤ After the first two games of the Western Conference Finals, fans outside of Oklahoma were writing off the Thunder. They were dominated by the Spurs in the first two games, losing by a combined 52 points! The Thunder won the next two games, however. Finally, a Game 6 overtime win sent the Spurs back to their second-straight NBA Finals.

➤ The Miami Heat made it four trips in a row to the Finals (the most since 1985), and continued their drive for a "threepeat."

George (right) led the Pacers over the Bulls.

2014 NBA Finals

GAME 1
San Antonio 110, Miami 95

The air conditioning in AT&T Center Arena wasn't working, but the Spurs were. The Heat couldn't handle the heat in the building. **LeBron James** had to leave during the fourth quarter after overheating. His absence let the Spurs take a lead they didn't give up.

GAME 2
Miami 98, San Antonio 96

LeBron James made up for missing part of Game 1 by pouring in 35 points. This was a close game, with the teams tied at halftime and the Spurs ahead by one at the end of the third quarter. A late three-pointer by **Chris Bosh** put Miami in front for good.

GAME 3
San Antonio 111, Miami 92

The Spurs put on one of the best shooting performances in NBA history and the Heat could not recover. San Antonio made 76 percent of its shots in the first half, the

The Spurs' Big Three took home NBA title Number Five.

highest percentage ever in a Finals game. **Kawhi Leonard** was an unexpected star for the Spurs, scoring a game-high 29 points.

GAME 4
San Antonio 107, Miami 86

For the first time since 2011, the Heat lost two straight playoff games at home. Leonard was the top scorer again. The Spurs held as much as a 25-point game in romping to within one game of another NBA title.

GAME 5
San Antonio 104, Miami 87

San Antonio won its fifth NBA title, led by center **Tim Duncan** and guards **Tony Parker** and **Manu Ginobili**. The Spurs came back from an early 16-point deficit.

❝There is no other way to say it. They played great basketball, and we couldn't respond to it.❞

— MIAMI COACH ERIK SPOELSTRA

NBA Awards

FINALLY...K.D.!

Watching **Kevin Durant** of the Thunder rack up the points, most fans say, "Wow!" Watching him accept his long-awaited first NBA MVP award, fans just said, "Awwww!" Durant tearfully thanked his mother, along with teammates, coaches, and fans, when he got the award in May. He even thanked the team trainer! Durant got all but six first-place votes after leading the NBA in scoring for the fourth time in five seasons. His 32.0 points per game average was the highest in the NBA in eight seasons. Durant also became the first scoring champ to grab the MVP trophy since **Allen Iverson** did so in 2001.

NBA AWARDS

SIXTH MAN	**Jamal Crawford,** Clippers
MOST IMPROVED	**Goran Dragic,** Suns
TOP DEFENDER	**Joakim Noah,** Bulls
ROOKIE OF THE YEAR	**Michael Carter-Williams,** 76ers
COMMUNITY ASSIST AWARD	**Stephen Curry,** Warriors
ALL-STAR GAME MVP	**Kyrie Irving,** Cavaliers

NBA Stat Leaders

Most NBA stats are ranked "per game" (pg). That is, the numbers here are the average each player had for each game he played.

32.0 POINTS (PPG)
Kevin Durant, Thunder

◀◀◀ 10.7 ASSISTS (APG)
Chris Paul, Clippers

5.4 OFF. REBOUNDS (ORPG)
Andre Drummond, Pistons

13.6 REBOUNDS (RPG)
DeAndre Jordan, Clippers

2.5 STEALS (SPG)
Chris Paul, Clippers

2.8 BLOCKS (BPG)
Anthony Davis, Pelicans

67.6 FG PCT.
DeAndre Jordan, Clippers

94.0 FT PCT.
Brian Roberts, Pelicans

127

That's how many games in a row that Atlanta's **Kyle Korver** made at least one three-point bucket, a new NBA record. He also ended up leading the NBA in three-point percentage, making 47.2 percent of his "treys."

In The Paint

Scoring Streak!

Turn him on and watch him score! Oklahoma City's **Kevin Durant**, on his way to his first

MVP, put on an amazing scoring show. In January, his run of 12 straight games with 30 or more points ended. During the season, he also had a run of 41 straight games with 25 or more points; that's the third-longest such streak of all time. By the time the overworked NBA scoreboards were shut down, Durant had poured in a total of 2,593 points. That was the second-highest total in more than 24 seasons!

◀◀◀ A Busy All-Star

Portland guard **Damian Lillard** probably wore out his sneakers during the 2014 NBA All-Star Weekend. First, he played in the Rising Stars Challenge, a game for younger players. Then he was a contestant in the skills contest, the three-point shootout, and even the dunk-off! Then he scored nine points in the All-Star Game itself! Lillard probably needed a break from the All-Star break!

A MESS IN L.A.

Other than the NBA Finals, the biggest news in the NBA for the past year came out of Los Angeles. In April 2014, the owner of the L.A. Clippers, **Donald Sterling**, was heard making racist comments on tape. Within days, calls for his removal came from everywhere. NBA Commissioner **Adam Silver** banned Sterling from the league and began a process to force him to sell the team. Before that could happen, however, Sterling's wife sold the team for an amazing $2 billion! The new owner is **Steve Ballmer**, who made his fortune helping to build Microsoft. For Clippers fans, it's a new beginning after a troubling period.

Bad News for Pacers Fans

In July, NBA fans were shocked by a gruesome injury to Indiana Pacers star **Paul George**. While playing for Team USA in a warmup before the World Championships, George landed badly after jumping. Both bones in his lower leg were broken. After surgery, George was expected to recover, but it will take a long time. The rising superstar will miss the entire 2014–15 season, and maybe even more time after that. Some people thought that NBA stars might choose not to play for national teams because of this risk of injury. In fact, several other stars pulled out of the 2014 World Cup of Basketball while they nursed minor injuries. However, NBA officials said they and the league still supported the national team.

5x3 Here's one you can amaze your friends with. What NBA superstar had the most triple-doubles in 2013–14? (That means reaching double digits in three stat categories in one game.) **LeBron**? **K.D.**? **Kobe**? Nope, **Lance Stephenson**, a rising young star who signed with Charlotte for 2014, had five!

NBA Draft: TOP 10 PICKS

NO.	TEAM	PLAYER, POSITION, COLLEGE
1.	**Cavaliers***	**ANDREW WIGGINS, G,** Kansas
2.	**Bucks**	**JABARI PARKER, F,** Duke
3.	**76ers**	**JOEL EMBIID, C,** Kansas
4.	**Magic**	**AARON GORDON, F,** Arizona
5.	**Jazz**	**DANTE EXUM, G,** Australia
6.	**Celtics**	**MARCUS SMART, G,** Oklahoma State
7.	**Lakers**	**JULIUS RANDLE, F,** Kentucky
8.	**Kings**	**NIK STAUSKAS, G,** Michigan
9.	**Hornets**	**NOAH VONLEH, F,** Indiana
10.	**76ers****	**ELFRID PAYTON, G,** Louisiana-Lafeyette

*Traded to Timberwolves. **Traded to Magic

2013 WNBA

Griner flew in the WNBA in 2013.

The big news in the WNBA for the 2013 season was the arrival of an exciting trio of rookies. After dominating college basketball for years, **Britney Griner** joined the Phoenix Mercury. Fans everywhere were excited to see what this shot-blocking, lane-clogging, slam-dunking talent could do. She certainly made a splash in her debut game, dunking twice, a rare feat in the WNBA. The rest of her season was more of a struggle, however, as she battled injuries. Phoenix made the playoffs, however, and Griner made the game- and series-winning shot in Game 3 of the first round against the L.A. Sparks.

While Griner got the headlines, another rookie got the wins. The Chicago Sky made Delaware star **Elena Della Donne** their first pick in the draft and she paid off big-time. The Sky led the Eastern Conference and earned their first-ever playoff appearance. How good was Della Donne? She won each of the four Rookie of the Month awards, and was a unanimous selection as WNBA Rookie of the Year.

Another top rookie was **Skylar Diggins**, the former Notre Dame guard, who joined the Tulsa Shock. Even her all-around talents could not keep Tulsa out of the basement, however.

Back at the top, the Minnesota Lynx continued a great run of success, earning their third straight trip to the WNBA Finals. **Maya Moore** continued her rise as one of the WNBA's best players ever, winning another scoring title.

2013 AWARDS AND LEADERS

WNBA MVP: **Candace Parker**, Los Angeles
ROOKIE OF THE YEAR: **Elena Delle Donne**, Chicago
DEFENSIVE PLAYER OF THE YEAR: **Sylvia Fowles**, Chicago
SCORING: **Angel McCoughtry**, Atlanta, 21.6 ppg
REBOUNDS: **Sylvia Fowles**, Chicago, 11.5 rpg
ASSISTS: **Danielle Robinson**, San Antonio, 6.7 apg

2013 WNBA FINALS

The WNBA Finals were more of the same from the regular season: The Lynx dominating the action. They swept the first two rounds of the playoffs, then kept it up in the Finals. This was a rematch of the 2011 WNBA Finals, and the result was the same: Minnesota on top.

GAME 1 Lynx 84, Dream 59

Minnesota came into this year's WNBA Finals knowing they had come close a year earlier, losing in the Finals to the Fever. Led by superstar **Maya Moore**, the Lynx started strong and never let up. They led after the first quarter, but started the second with a 15–0 run. It was never close after that and they cruised to an easy win.

"Moore" of the same in the finals.

GAME 2 Lynx 88, Dream 63

It was "**Moore**" of the same in Game 2, as the star poured in 14 more points. But she had a lot of help. Five Lynx players had at least 10 points each, with **Seimone Augustus** leading the way with 20. Minnesota was ahead by as many as 31 points.

2013 WNBA FINAL STANDINGS

REGULAR SEASON

EASTERN CONFERENCE		WESTERN CONFERENCE	
Chicago	24-10	Minnesota	26-8
Atlanta	17-17	Los Angeles	24-10
Washington	17-17	Phoenix	19-15
Indiana	16-18	Seattle	17-17
New York	11-23	San Antonio	12-22
Connecticut	10-24	Tulsa	11-23

GAME 3 Lynx 86, Dream 77

Atlanta finally showed up in Game 3, at least for the first half. But in the second half, **Moore** and **Rebekkah Brunson** turned on the jets and the Lynx ran away with another WNBA championship. Combined with earlier visits, Atlanta ran their Finals record to a rotten 0–10. Moore was the leading scorer in this game and was named WNBA Finals MVP.

Stat Stuff

NBA CHAMPIONS

2013–14 **San Antonio**	2007–08 **Boston**	1992–93 **Chicago**
2012–13 **Miami**	2006–07 **San Antonio**	1991–92 **Chicago**
2011–12 **Miami**	2005–06 **Miami**	1990–91 **Chicago**
2010–11 **Dallas**	2004–05 **San Antonio**	1989–90 **Detroit**
2009–10 **L.A. Lakers**	2003–04 **Detroit**	1988–89 **Detroit**
2008–09 **L.A. Lakers**	2002–03 **San Antonio**	1987–88 **L.A. Lakers**
	2001–02 **L.A. Lakers**	1986–87 **L.A. Lakers**
	2000–01 **L.A. Lakers**	1985–86 **Boston**
	1999–00 **L.A. Lakers**	1984–85 **L.A. Lakers**
	1998–99 **San Antonio**	1983–84 **Boston**
	1997–98 **Chicago**	1982–83 **Philadelphia**
	1996–97 **Chicago**	1981–82 **L.A. Lakers**
	1995–96 **Chicago**	1980–81 **Boston**
	1994–95 **Houston**	1979–80 **L.A. Lakers**
	1993–94 **Houston**	1978–79 **Seattle**

Bill Russell (6) led the Celtics to an amazing 11 NBA titles.

1977–78 **Washington**	1959–60 **Boston**	1952–53 **Minneapolis**
1976–77 **Portland**	1958–59 **Boston**	1951–52 **Minneapolis**
1975–76 **Boston**	1957–58 **St. Louis**	1950–51 **Rochester**
1974–75 **Golden State**	1956–57 **Boston**	1949–50 **Minneapolis**
1973–74 **Boston**	1955–56 **Philadelphia**	1948–49 **Minneapolis**
1972–73 **New York**	1954–55 **Syracuse**	1947–48 **Baltimore**
1971–72 **L.A. Lakers**	1953–54 **Minneapolis**	1946–47 **Philadelphia**
1970–71 **Milwaukee**		
1969–70 **New York**		

WNBA CHAMPIONS

1968–69 **Boston**	2013 **Minnesota**	2004 **Seattle**
1967–68 **Boston**	2012 **Indiana**	2003 **Detroit**
1966–67 **Philadelphia**	2011 **Minnesota**	2002 **Los Angeles**
1965–66 **Boston**	2010 **Seattle**	2001 **Los Angeles**
1964–65 **Boston**	2009 **Phoenix**	2000 **Houston**
1963–64 **Boston**	2008 **Detroit**	1999 **Houston**
1962–63 **Boston**	2007 **Phoenix**	1998 **Houston**
1961–62 **Boston**	2006 **Detroit**	1997 **Houston**
1960–61 **Boston**	2005 **Sacramento**	

NHL

HAPPY . . . AND NOT

Kings defenseman Alec Martinez is about to start the celebration after his double-overtime goal gave his team a win in Game 5 . . . and the Stanley Cup championship. Rangers goalie Henrik Lundqvist does not feel the same way.

Crown the Kings

Ovechkin shows off his powerful shooting skill.

Atlantic and Metropolitan divisions. Also, the Detroit Red Wings and Columbus Blue Jackets moved to the East.

A new power emerged in the West when the Colorado Avalanche played inspired hockey under their fiery new coach, **Patrick Roy**. They also got outstanding play from goalie **Semyon Valarmov**. The Avalanche went from the second-worst record of 2013 to the NHL's third-best record in 2014.

Another new powerhouse rose in the East. The Tampa Bay Lightning certainly struck in 2013–2014, because the team made a loud noise behind the offensive might of center **Martin St. Louis**, a group of excellent young rookie forwards, and lanky (6-foot-7) goalie **Ben Bishop**. The Lightning finished with the third best record in the East.

Some teams surprised fans with their climb to the top, others startled people with a bit of a tumble. The Chicago Blackhawks, defending Stanley Cup champions, picked up an impressive 107 points. That was only good enough for fifth place in the powerful Western Conference.

A fter a lockout-shortened 2013 season, hockey fans were hungry for the start of the full, 82-game, 2013–2014 season. They got what they were hoping for in great races, new faces, and plenty of star power.

The season had a different look, after the NHL moved teams around for the first time since 1998. The Western Conference was split into the Pacific and Central Divisions. The Eastern Conference had the

As for star power, Washington Capitals winger **Alexander Ovechkin** and Tampa Bay Lightning center **Steven Stamkos** were expected to battle it out in a goal-scoring race, but Stamkos's season was derailed by a broken leg. Ovechkin ended up as the league's leading goal-scorer for the fourth time, finishing with 51 goals.

The season also featured spectacular rookies. One of the driving forces behind the great play of the Avalanche was speedy center **Nathan MacKinnon**. MacKinnon had a 13-game point-scoring streak, the longest by an 18-year-old. That broke **Wayne Gretzky's** record from 1979–80.

As MacKinnon helped revive the Avalanche, two other rookies jumpstarted the Lightning. Forward **Ondrej Palat** led all rookies in plus-minus rating, while center **Tyler Johnson** scored 24 goals to set a Lightning rookie record. Other outstanding members of the freshman class included center **Boone Jenner** of the Blue Jackets; **Hampus Lindholm**, the Anaheim Ducks' quick-moving defenseman; and one of the slickest puck handlers and goal scorers around, San Jose Sharks center **Tomas Hertl**.

The Stanley Cup playoffs (page 122) included some of the most dramatic series in recent years. In the end, a familiar team captured another kind of crown!

RULE CHANGES

For the 2013–14 season, the NHL made some key rule changes. First, the nets on the goal were made four inches shallower. This gives goalies more room to move, but it also allows offensive players more space to set up creative plays from behind the net.

When a player shoots the puck across both the center red line and the opposing team's goal line, if the puck is untouched, it's icing. This season, the icing rule got a twist. A change was made to cut down on collisions and injuries from players racing to the puck. Under the old system, if the puck was first touched by a player on the team that iced it, the icing was waved off. The new rule tells officials to stop play when an official judges that defender would win a race to the puck.

FINAL STANDINGS

EASTERN CONFERENCE

ATLANTIC DIVISION	W	L	OTL	PTS
1 Boston	54	19	9	117
2 Tampa Bay	46	27	9	101
3 Montreal	46	28	8	100
4 Detroit	39	28	15	93
5 Ottawa	37	31	14	88
6 Toronto	38	36	8	84
7 Florida	29	45	8	66
8 Buffalo	21	51	10	52

METROPOLITAN DIV.	W	L	OTL	PTS
1 Pittsburgh	51	24	7	109
2 NY Rangers	45	31	6	96
3 Philadelphia	42	30	10	94
4 Columbus	43	32	7	93
5 Washington	38	30	14	90
6 New Jersey	35	29	18	88
7 Carolina	36	35	11	83
8 NY Islanders	34	37	11	79

WESTERN CONFERENCE

CENTRAL DIVISION	W	L	OTL	PTS
1 Colorado	52	22	8	112
2 St. Louis	52	23	7	111
3 Chicago	46	21	15	107
4 Minnesota	43	27	12	98
5 Dallas	40	31	11	91
6 Nashville	38	32	12	88
7 Winnipeg	37	35	10	84

PACIFIC DIVISION	W	L	OTL	PTS
1 Anaheim	54	20	8	116
2 San Jose	51	22	9	111
3 Los Angeles	46	28	8	100
4 Phoenix	37	30	15	89
5 Vancouver	36	35	11	83
6 Calgary	35	40	7	77
7 Edmonton	29	44	9	67

NHL Playoffs

The big surprises in the playoffs were in the Eastern Conference, where all eyes were on the top-seeded Boston Bruins and the high-scoring Pittsburgh Penguins. Both advanced easily in the first round.

In the West, the Los Angeles Kings, Stanley Cup winners just two seasons ago, provided some drama in the first round by coming back from a 3–2 deficit to knock out the San Jose Sharks. It was just the third time in NHL history a team had done that. The Minnesota Wild upset the Colorado Avalanche in seven games.

In the second round, the New York Rangers stunned the Penguins, overcoming a 3–1 Penguins series lead. They did it while holding league-leading scorer **Sidney Crosby** to just one goal. The Montreal Canadiens tossed their archrival Bruins in seven games. Out West, the Kings did it again, coming back from a 3–0 hole to beat the Anaheim Ducks.

The Conference finals saw the Rangers triumph over the Canadiens in six games, but Kings fans had to bite their nails yet again. This time the Chicago Blackhawks came back from a 3–1 deficit to force a Game 7 in Chicago. With the Blackhawks leading late in

To make the Stanley Cup Finals, the Rangers (in blue) overcame the Canadiens.

the game, Kings forward **Marion Gaborik** tied it with just 7:17 left. In overtime, Kings defenseman **Alec Martinez** lofted a shot that hit a Blackhawks player before settling in the back of the net.

THE FINALS

Before the Kings met the Rangers in the Finals, both teams had dug themselves out of deep holes in the playoffs. And both had goaltenders (**Jonathan Quick** for the Kings and **Henrik Lundqvist** for the Rangers) among the league's best.

The Rangers took two-goal leads in each of the first two games in Los Angeles. But the Kings showed their toughness by winning Game 1 on an overtime goal by **Justin Williams**. Then they took Game 2 in double OT.

The Kings pushed their advantage to 3–0 by winning in New York, thanks to a superb 32-save shutout by Quick. The Rangers answered with a win and a brilliant game by Lundqvist, who stopped 40 shots.

The Rangers took the lead again in Game 5 in Los Angeles. The Kings tied the game in the third period on a goal by **Marian Gaborik**. Deciding a winner took two overtimes, with both teams hitting posts and their goalies making amazing saves.

Finally, LA defender **Alec Martinez** punched home the game-winning goal to give the Kings the Stanley Cup for the second time in three seasons.

PLAYOFF RESULTS
(Games won in parentheses)

FIRST ROUND

EASTERN CONFERENCE

Boston OVER Detroit (4-1)
Montreal OVER Tampa Bay (4-0)
Pittsburgh OVER Columbus (4-2)
NY Rangers OVER Philadelphia (4-3)

WESTERN CONFERENCE

Minnesota OVER Colorado (4-3)
Chicago OVER St. Louis (4-2)
Anaheim OVER Dallas (4-2)
Los Angeles OVER San Jose (4-3)

CONFERENCE SEMIFINALS

EASTERN CONFERENCE

Montreal OVER Boston (4-3)
NY Rangers OVER Pittsburgh (4-3)

WESTERN CONFERENCE

Chicago OVER Minnesota (4-2)
Los Angeles OVER Anaheim (4-3)

CONFERENCE FINALS

EASTERN CONFERENCE

NY Rangers OVER Montreal (4-2)

WESTERN CONFERENCE

Los Angeles OVER Chicago (4-3)

STANLEY CUP FINALS

Los Angeles OVER NY Rangers (4-1)

Hockey Highlights

Pulling the Goalie

Patrick Roy was rarely pulled from the net when he was the superstar netminder for the Canadiens and Avalanche. Now, as Colorado's coach, he sees things differently. When teams are trailing and there is about 1:30 left in the game, they typically take their goaltender off the ice to put on an extra forward. But several times during the season and playoffs, Roy pulled his goalie with more than two minutes left, in one game with 4:46 on the clock, to try for the tie. It's a gutsy move—and a successful one—so other coaches are now trying it.

Take It Outside

The Winter Classic has been so successful for the NHL that they decided more would definitely be better. In the official 2014 Winter Classic on New Year's Day, the host Detroit Red Wings were beat by the Toronto Maple Leafs in a shootout. The game took place in front of a huge crowd at the Big House, the University of Michigan's football stadium in Ann Arbor. But there were four other outdoor games, dubbed the Stadium Series. The Los Angeles Kings hosted the Anaheim Ducks at Dodger Stadium, the New York Rangers faced the New Jersey

So Long, Selanne

On May 16, 2014, Anaheim Ducks forward **Teemu Selanne** skated in his final NHL game. He retired after one of the best careers of recent decades. In his 21 seasons in the NHL, he played 1,451 games, won the Calder, Rocket Richard, and Masterton Trophies, and one Stanley Cup (2007). He also played in 10 All-Star games. Selanne is the highest-scoring player from Finland in NHL history. Selanne also helped his nation win four Olympic hockey medals. His 43 points are the most ever in Olympic hockey history.

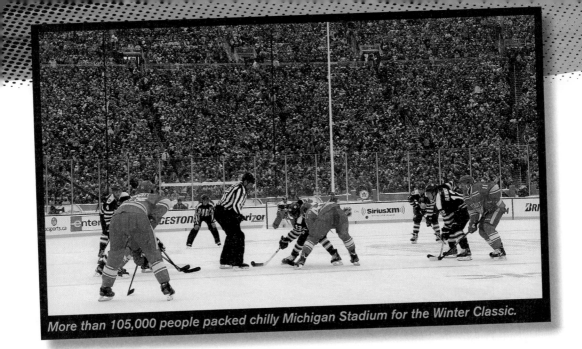

More than 105,000 people packed chilly Michigan Stadium for the Winter Classic.

Devils and the New York Islanders at Yankee Stadium, and the Chicago Blackhawks and the Pittsburgh Penguins faced off at Soldier Field. The Heritage Classic also returned, with the Ottawa Senators playing the Vancouver Canucks at BC Place.

Where's My Passport?

Goaltender Kristers Gudlevskis may be hockey's most well-traveled player. In 2013, he became the first hockey player to play in the ECHL, AHL, NHL, Olympic Games, and IIHF World Championships . . . all in the same season! (The ECHL and AHL are minor pro hockey leagues in Canada.) Gudlevskis spent most of the season in the AHL, but won national attention when he stopped 55 shots for the Latvian National Team in a 2–1 loss to Canada during the 2014 Olympics in Sochi, Russia. The jet-lagged goalie made one start for the Tampa Bay Lightning, a 3–2 win.

Besting Gretzky

It's not often that someone breaks one of Wayne Gretzky's records, but Taylor Hall did. Gretzky held the Edmonton Oilers record for the fastest two goals in franchise history, scoring two goals nine seconds apart in 1981. On October 17, 2013, Hall scored twice in eight seconds, beating Gretzky's mark by a second.

Family Draft Day

The 2014 NHL Entry Draft featured a lot of family ties. The second overall pick, Sam Reinhart, became the third member of his family to be selected in the first round. His older brother, Griffin, went to the New York Islanders in 2012, and his father, Paul, was drafted by the Atlanta Flames in 1979. His oldest brother, Max, was selected by the Calgary Flames in 2010. Three other first-round draft picks had family ties to current or former NHLers as well. Pucks run in the family!

2013-14 Awards

Hart Trophy (MVP), and
Ted Lindsay Award (Outstanding Player as Voted by the Players), and
Art Ross Trophy (Most Points)
SIDNEY CROSBY,
Pittsburgh Penguins

Conn Smythe Trophy
(Stanley Cup Playoffs MVP)
JUSTIN WILLIAMS, LA Kings

" This really means a lot, to be recognized by the guys that you compete against every night. "

— SIDNEY CROSBY ON
WINNING HIS THIRD LINDSAY AWARD

Vezina Trophy (Best Goaltender)
TUUKKA RASK, Boston Bruins

William Jennings Trophy
(Goalie with Fewest Goals Scored Against Him)
JONATHAN QUICK, LA Kings

James Norris Memorial Trophy
(Best Defenseman)
DUNCAN KEITH, Chicago Blackhawks

Frank J. Selke Trophy
(Best Defensive Forward)
PATRICE BERGERON, Boston Bruins

Calder Memorial Trophy
(Best Rookie)
◀◀◀ NATHAN MACKINNON,
Colorado Avalanche

Lady Byng Memorial Trophy
(Most Gentlemanly Player)
RYAN O'REILLY, Colorado Avalanche

Jack Adams Award (Best Coach)
PATRICK ROY, Colorado Avalanche

General Manager of the Year
BOB MURRAY, Anaheim Ducks

2013-14 Stat Leaders

104 POINTS
Sidney Crosby, Penguins ▶▶▶

51 GOALS
Alex Ovechkin, Capitals

68 ASSISTS
Sidney Crosby, Penguins

1.65 GOALS AGAINST AVG.
Josh Harding, Wild

.933 SAVE PERCENTAGE
Josh Harding, Wild

41 WINS/GOALIE
Semyon Varlamov, Avalanche

7 SHUTOUTS
Tuukka Rask, Bruins

39 SHOOTOUT SAVES
Ben Bishop, Lightning

+39 PLUS/MINUS
David Krejci, Bruins

1,015 FACEOFFS WON
Patrice Bergeron, Bruins

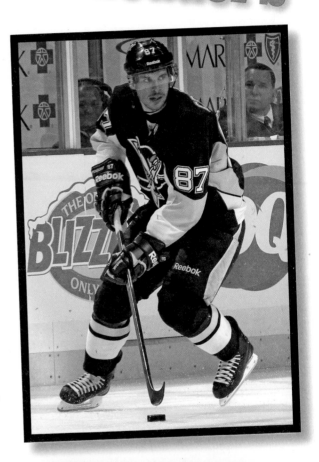

122

That's Penguins center (and Devils wing) Jaromir Jagr's new career record for game-winning goals. He knocked Gordie "Mr. Hockey" Howe out of the books!

Stanley Cup Champions

2013–14	**Los Angeles Kings**		1987–88	**Edmonton Oilers**
2012–13	**Chicago Blackhawks**		1986–87	**Edmonton Oilers**
2011–12	**Los Angeles Kings**		1985–86	**Montreal Canadiens**
2010–11	**Boston Bruins**		1984–85	**Edmonton Oilers**
2009–10	**Chicago Blackhawks**		1983–84	**Edmonton Oilers**
2008–09	**Pittsburgh Penguins**		1982–83	**New York Islanders**
2007–08	**Detroit Red Wings**		1981–82	**New York Islanders**
2006–07	**Anaheim Ducks**		1980–81	**New York Islanders**
2005–06	**Carolina Hurricanes**		1979–80	**New York Islanders**
2004–05	No champion (Lockout)		1978–79	**Montreal Canadiens**
2003–04	**Tampa Bay Lightning**		1977–78	**Montreal Canadiens**
2002–03	**New Jersey Devils**		1976–77	**Montreal Canadiens**
2001–02	**Detroit Red Wings**		1975–76	**Montreal Canadiens**
2000–01	**Colorado Avalanche**		1974–75	**Philadelphia Flyers**
1999–00	**New Jersey Devils**		1973–74	**Philadelphia Flyers**
1998–99	**Dallas Stars**		1972–73	**Montreal Canadiens**
1997–98	**Detroit Red Wings**		1971–72	**Boston Bruins**
1996–97	**Detroit Red Wings**		1970–71	**Montreal Canadiens**
1995–96	**Colorado Avalanche**		1969–70	**Boston Bruins**
1994–95	**New Jersey Devils**		1968–69	**Montreal Canadiens**
1993–94	**New York Rangers**		1967–68	**Montreal Canadiens**
1992–93	**Montreal Canadiens**		1966–67	**Toronto Maple Leafs**
1991–92	**Pittsburgh Penguins**		1965–66	**Montreal Canadiens**
1990–91	**Pittsburgh Penguins**		1964–65	**Montreal Canadiens**
1989–90	**Edmonton Oilers**		1963–64	**Toronto Maple Leafs**
1988–89	**Calgary Flames**		1962–63	**Toronto Maple Leafs**

1961–62	**Toronto Maple Leafs**
1960–61	**Chicago Blackhawks**
1959–60	**Montreal Canadiens**
1958–59	**Montreal Canadiens**
1957–58	**Montreal Canadiens**
1956–57	**Montreal Canadiens**
1955–56	**Montreal Canadiens**
1954–55	**Detroit Red Wings**
1953–54	**Detroit Red Wings**
1952–53	**Montreal Canadiens**
1951–52	**Detroit Red Wings**
1950–51	**Toronto Maple Leafs**
1949–50	**Detroit Red Wings**
1948–49	**Toronto Maple Leafs**
1947–48	**Toronto Maple Leafs**
1946–47	**Toronto Maple Leafs**
1945–46	**Montreal Canadiens**
1944–45	**Toronto Maple Leafs**
1943–44	**Montreal Canadiens**
1942–43	**Detroit Red Wings**
1941–42	**Toronto Maple Leafs**
1940–41	**Boston Bruins**
1939–40	**New York Rangers**
1938–39	**Boston Bruins**
1937–38	**Chicago Blackhawks**
1936–37	**Detroit Red Wings**
1935–36	**Detroit Red Wings**
1934–35	**Montreal Maroons**
1933–34	**Chicago Blackhawks**

MOST STANLEY CUP TITLES

Montreal Canadiens	**23**
Toronto Maple Leafs	**13**
Detroit Red Wings	**11**
Boston Bruins	**6**
Edmonton Oilers	**5**

1932–33	**New York Rangers**
1931–32	**Toronto Maple Leafs**
1930–31	**Montreal Canadiens**
1929–30	**Montreal Canadiens**
1928–29	**Boston Bruins**
1927–28	**New York Rangers**
1926–27	**Ottawa Senators**
1925–26	**Montreal Maroons**
1924–25	**Victoria Cougars**
1923–24	**Montreal Canadiens**
1922–23	**Ottawa Senators**
1921–22	**Toronto St. Patricks**
1920–21	**Ottawa Senators**
1919–20	**Ottawa Senators**
1918–19	No decision
1917–18	**Toronto Arenas**

NASCAR

HERE WE GO AGAIN!

Jimmie Johnson dominated the 2013 Chase for the Cup and zoomed away with his sixth career NASCAR Sprint Cup championship. Never the flashiest driver or the most controversial, he just wins . . . again and again. Johnson went for a record-tying seventh title in 2014.

Jimmie Johnson (48) saved his best for last, winning late in the season to clinch the Cup.

The 2013 Chase

NASCAR racing is a bumper-busting, fast-moving, thrill-a-minute ride from the Daytona 500 to the final race of the season. Or at least that's what fans and NASCAR owners hope. In 2013, they all got their wish. A season of great performances (and not a few wild wrecks) led to a final-round Chase for the Cup that was one of the most exciting in years. As **Jimmie Johnson**, who had already won five NASCAR titles, said, "This will all come down to the last lap of the last race at Homestead."

Johnson himself was not the favorite heading into the Chase. As the Chase began, **Matt Kenseth** was the man to beat. He had won five races during the regular season and led the points race. A late-season controversy led to a shuffling of the Chase spots (see page 134), too, making the field 13 drivers for the first time.

When the Chase began, it was business as usual. Kenseth won the first two races to lengthen his lead. But one thing about Johnson: You can't count him out! He won

CHASE FOR THE CUP

2013 FINAL STANDINGS

1. **Jimmie JOHNSON**
2. **Matt KENSETH**
3. **Kevin HARVICK**
4. **Kyle BUSCH**
5. **Dale EARNHARDT JR.**
6. **Jeff GORDON**
7. **Clint BOWYER**
8. **Joey LOGANO**
9. **Greg BIFFLE**
10. **Kurt BUSCH**

7.89

That's how many MILLIONS of dollars **Jimmie Johnson** took home for winning the 2013 NASCAR Sprint Cup title!

win the big trophy. "JJ" would have to race his best to make sure that didn't happen again.

With millions watching on TV and thousands packing the sunny stands, Johnson tried to hold to his overall lead. Kenseth tried to catch him.

He didn't.

The veteran drove smoothly and safely, finishing ninth overall. That was enough to give him his sixth NASCAR Sprint Cup championship. He trails only the great **Richard Petty** and **Dale Earnhardt Sr.**, who each won seven times.

the third race, the AAA 400, and climbed closer. After that, he battled back to tie Kenseth in the points race. At Talladega, Johnson was racing to catch Kenseth, but tire trouble slowed him and he was still trailing after five Chase races.

But he kept at it, gaining points in the next few races. Finally, by winning his second Chase race at Texas, Johnson broke a tie with Kenseth and took the overall lead with two races left. That put Kenseth in the position of the chaser, not the chasee! But Kenseth couldn't gain points at Phoenix, setting up a last-race sprint for the title, just as Johnson predicted.

He hoped that history would not repeat itself. In 2012, Johnson had held the lead late in the Chase, but watched as **Brad Keselowski** zoomed by to

Matt Kenseth led with seven tire-smoking victories in 2013.

Around the Track: 2013

to the Chase. Gordon was put back in thanks in part to shenanigans by two other teams. The NASCAR chief made it clear that he was in charge!

◄◄◄ It Worked!

NASCAR introduced a whole new line of cars for the 2013 season. The "Gen-6" cars were supposed to even the playing field, er . . . track! When the final races were over, the experiment proved to be a success. Average finishes were the closest they had been in eight seasons. And in 20 of the races, the margin of victory was less than a second! Plus, drivers set new track qualifying times 19 times! Looks like Gen-6 is here to stay, racing fans!

Last-Minute Shift

The race for the Chase got a bit complicated after the final race of the 2013 season. As the results stood, it looked like Jeff Gordon was out, along with Ryan Newman. But NASCAR chairman Brian France thought otherwise. He and his experts investigated a wreck in the Richmond race and other issues. They decided that other racers and teams had broken the rules to help their teammates. When the dust settled, France had kicked Martin Truex out of the Chase, fined his team money and points, and added Newman back

Truck Series Results

The most popular "car" in America is a pickup truck, the Ford F150. So it's no surprise that racing fans like to see pickups race, too. In 2013, Matt Crafton only won one race in the NASCAR Camping World Truck Series, but he was the most consistent driver of the season. He finished in the top 10 19 times in 22 races. That gave him enough points to finish ahead of Ty Dillon.

GEARS AND WHEELS

- At the start of the 2013 season, **Danica Patrick** became the first female driver to earn the pole position, which she did in the famous Daytona 500.
- **Tony Stewart** missed 15 races after breaking his leg in a crash racing sprint cars on dirt.
- Return to dirt: For the first time since 1970, a NASCAR race was held on a dirt track. The event was in the NASCAR Camping World Truck Series.

A Milestone Win ▶▶▶

One of NASCAR's biggest aims in the coming years is to increase its diversity. That is, they want to find ways to make sure that people of all backgrounds—not just those from the sport's white Southern roots—find a home in the NASCAR world. In 2013, for the first time since **Wendell Scott** won in 1963, an African-American driver captured a major NASCAR race. **Darrell Wallace Jr.** won the Kroger 200 Camping World Truck Series race at Martinsville.

NATIONWIDE SERIES

NASCAR's second-level racing series turned in some first-rate racing in 2013. Some of the biggest winners were familiar names from the Sprint Cup level. **Kyle Busch** won a season-high 12 races, while fellow Sprint star **Brad Keselowski** won seven. But since those guys are not eligible to win the season title, the battle was one for a couple of NASCAR family members. **Austin Dillon** ended up only three points ahead of **Sam Hornish Jr.** to win the overall title. Dillon won without capturing a checkered flag, but he did have 22 top-10 finishes.

"We congratulate Darrell Wallace Jr. on his first national series victory, one that will be remembered as a remarkable moment in our sport's history,"

—BRIAN FRANCE, NASCAR chairman and CEO

Around the Track: 2014

Dale at Daytona

His dad, **Dale Sr.**, won this race in 1998. **Dale Earnhardt Jr.** won it in 2004, but had gone a long time without a big win. In fact, he had three second-place finishes since then. He changed that in February—and put himself in the Chase race— by winning his second Daytona 500. Thanks to rain delays, it took a whole day to finish the race, but at the end, Junior was the man in front.

KURT BUSCH
DOES THE DOUBLE

Kurt Busch must *reeeallly* like driving. On Memorial Day, he became the fourth driver to perform an amazing double. In the afternoon, he competed in the Indy 500 (he finished sixth) on the Indy Car circuit. He jumped into a helicopter and then in a private plane and zoomed south to North Carolina. Without much more than a sandwich and a drink, he then hopped into his NASCAR ride and started in the Coca-Cola 600. A blown engine on lap 271 ended his long day a bit short . . . but a tired driver probably didn't mind!

WILD START

In the first 12 races of the 2014 NASCAR season, there were nine different winners! NASCAR stats showed that lead changes in races were up more than 45 percent in the first half of the season. Drivers were no longer hanging back to pick up points . . . they were going for the checkered flag! With a win almost guaranteeing a spot in the Chase, that meant a whole garage full of drivers were already making their plans for the fall.

NO PRESSURE, KID

Austin Dillon is a fine young driver. He'll certainly be in the hunt for championships and race wins. But in 2014, he was in the spotlight for another reason. His car owner, **Richard Childress**, did something few thought would ever happen: Childress put No. 3 on a car again. That number, which his team owns, belonged to the legendary **Dale Earnhardt Sr.**, who was killed during the 2001 Daytona 500. But Childress decided to bring it back and give it to Dillon. **Dale Earnhardt Jr.** gave his okay, but many fans were upset at the move. Childress has a special place for Dillon; Austin is his grandson!

Another familiar number found Victory Lane in 2014. No. 43 was made famous by **Richard Petty**, the all-time NASCAR champ with 200 race wins. At a rain-shortened Coke Zero 400, **Aric Almirola** steered No. 43 to the first victory for that car since 1999.

A WHOLE NEW CHASE

For the 2014 NASCAR season, the folks who run the show made some changes. In an effort to juice up interest in the sport—especially the year-end Chase for the Cup—new rules made the final race winner-take-all. Starting in 2014, one win during the season almost automatically qualifies a driver for the Chase. Up to 16 drivers earned spots based on wins; if more than 16 win races, points come into play. During the 10-race Chase, drivers will slowly be dropped out for poor finishes. The final race of the season pitted the top four remaining drivers. Whoever finishes highest at that race in Miami is the season champion.

Gordon's Favorite

The Brickyard 400 is one of NASCAR's most famous events. It is held at the Indianapolis Motor Speedway, the longtime home of the famous Indy 500 race. NASCAR has held races there for 20 years now, and **Jeff Gordon** has won 25 percent of them! He won his fifth Brickyard 400 in July. It was his second win of the year and added to his series-leading points total.

NASCAR Champions

Year	Driver	Make		Year	Driver	Make
2013	Jimmie Johnson	Chevrolet		1994	Dale Earnhardt Sr.	Chevrolet
2012	Brad Keselowski	Ford		1993	Dale Earnhardt Sr.	Chevrolet
2011	Tony Stewart	Chevrolet		1992	Alan Kulwicki	Ford
2010	Jimmie Johnson	Chevrolet		1991	Dale Earnhardt Sr.	Chevrolet
2009	Jimmie Johnson	Chevrolet		1990	Dale Earnhardt Sr.	Chevrolet
2008	Jimmie Johnson	Chevrolet		1989	Rusty Wallace	Pontiac
2007	Jimmie Johnson	Chevrolet		1988	Bill Elliott	Ford
2006	Jimmie Johnson	Chevrolet		1987	Dale Earnhardt Sr.	Chevrolet
2005	Tony Stewart	Chevrolet		1986	Dale Earnhardt Sr.	Chevrolet
2004	Kurt Busch	Ford		1985	Darrell Waltrip	Chevrolet
2003	Matt Kenseth	Ford		1984	Terry Labonte	Chevrolet
2002	Tony Stewart	Pontiac		1983	Bobby Allison	Buick
2001	Jeff Gordon	Chevrolet		1982	Darrell Waltrip	Buick
2000	Bobby Labonte	Pontiac		1981	Darrell Waltrip	Buick
1999	Dale Jarrett	Ford		1980	Dale Earnhardt Sr.	Chevrolet
1998	Jeff Gordon	Chevrolet		1979	Richard Petty	Chevrolet
1997	Jeff Gordon	Chevrolet		1978	Cale Yarborough	Oldsmobile
1996	Terry Labonte	Chevrolet		1977	Cale Yarborough	Chevrolet
1995	Jeff Gordon	Chevrolet		1976	Cale Yarborough	Chevrolet

1975	Richard Petty	Dodge		1961	Ned Jarrett	Chevrolet
1974	Richard Petty	Dodge		1960	Rex White	Chevrolet
1973	Benny Parsons	Chevrolet		1959	Lee Petty	Plymouth
1972	Richard Petty	Plymouth		1958	Lee Petty	Oldsmobile
1971	Richard Petty	Plymouth		1957	Buck Baker	Chevrolet
1970	Bobby Isaac	Dodge		1956	Buck Baker	Chrysler
1969	David Pearson	Ford		1955	Tim Flock	Chrysler
1968	David Pearson	Ford		1954	Lee Petty	Chrysler
1967	Richard Petty	Plymouth		1953	Herb Thomas	Hudson
1966	David Pearson	Dodge		1952	Tim Flock	Hudson
1965	Ned Jarrett	Ford		1951	Herb Thomas	Hudson
1964	Richard Petty	Plymouth		1950	Bill Rexford	Oldsmobile
1963	Joe Weatherly	Pontiac		1949	Red Byron	Oldsmobile
1962	Joe Weatherly	Pontiac				

2015 NASCAR HALL OF FAME CLASS

Meet the newest members of this exclusive club.

Bill Elliott: Driver who won 44 races on NASCAR's top level. Was 1988 NASCAR Champion. First driver to win the Winston Million, a $1-million dollar bonus. Also was named Most Popular Driver 16 times.

Fred Lorenzen: Driver who was one of the top racers in the 1960s.

Wendell Scott: Pioneer who was first African-American to win NASCAR race in 1963. Competed in nearly 500 races.

Joe Weatherly: Was the NASCAR champion back-to-back in 1962 and 1963. Won 25 races in his long career.

Rex White: Short-track specialist who won the 1960 NASCAR title.

OTHER MOTOR SPORTS

AUTO-LOCATOR
AUTO-LOCATOR

TOYOTARACING.COM

Buildings for R

www.ppclubricants.
500-772-582

GONE IN FOUR SECONDS!
Top Fuel dragsters run the shortest races in motor sports, but they are also among the fastest machines! Shawn Langdon captured the NHRA Top Fuel championship in 2013 with tire-smoking starts like this one. *Read about more drag racing on page 144.*

Formula 1

Thirteen was lucky for German racing star **Sebastian Vettel**. That's how many races he won during one of the most dominating seasons ever in Formula 1. Vettel claimed his fourth straight series championship, winning by more than 150 points over **Fernando Alonso**. He was so far ahead that he clinched the overall title with three races left.

"I'm speechless," said Vettel after he clinched in India. "I don't know what to say, I crossed the line and I was just empty. You want to think of something to say and I just can't. It has been an amazing season, the spirit in the team is great and it is a pleasure to jump in the car and drive."

After finishing third to start the season in Australia, Vettel won in Malaysia. From there he never took his foot off the gas.

4 Four-Time F1 Winners

Germany's **Sebastian Vettel** joined a select group when he won his fourth Formula 1 title in 2013. **Michael Schumacher** leads the way with seven. **Juan Manuel Fangio** had five. **Alain Prost**, like Vettel, had four.

He won in Bahrain and Canada to pad his growing lead. In July, he enjoyed home-track advantage as he won the German Grand Prix.

Two weeks after that race, he started a truly amazing streak. From the Belgian

Vettel put on a racing clinic in 2013, one of the most dominating F1 seasons ever.

FORMULA 1 GOES TO INDY!

The Indianapolis Motor Speedway is used to big-time racing. After all, they've held the Indy 500 there since 1911! But in 2014, Formula 1 made its debut at the historic track. Actually, the Indy Grand Prix was run on the road course that includes the Indy straightaway. The rest of the course snakes around the infield of the massive place. The start of the race was a bit shocking. Pole-sitter Sebastian Saavedra's car simply did not start when the green flag dropped. Other cars did, though, and as they tried to evade the stalled car, a big wreck sent several drivers out before the race really began. Simon Pagenaud managed to avoid all the damage, however. He took a late lead and held on for the victory.

Grand Prix in late August to the season-ending race in Brazil, he never lost a race. Nine straight trips to the top of the podium. His winning streak sounded like "Around the World in 80 Races": Belgium, Italy, Singapore, Korea, Japan, India, Abu Dhabi, Texas, and Brazil. It was the longest single-season winning streak in Formula 1 history. Only the great **Michael Schumacher** had also won as many as 13 races in one season, back in 2004. Oh, and the 397 points he racked up? Also, an all-time record.

Thirteen was pretty lucky indeed.

2013 F1 FINAL STANDINGS

PLACE/DRIVER	COUNTRY	TEAM	POINTS
1. **Sebastian VETTEL**	Germany	Infiniti Red Bull Racing	397
2. **Fernando ALONSO**	Spain	Scuderia Ferrari	242
3. **Mark WEBBER**	Australia	Infiniti Red Bull Racing	199
4. **Lewis HAMILTON**	Great Britain	Mercedes AMG Petronas	189
5. **Kimi RÄIKKÖNEN**	Finland	Lotus F1 Team	183

Drag Racing 2013

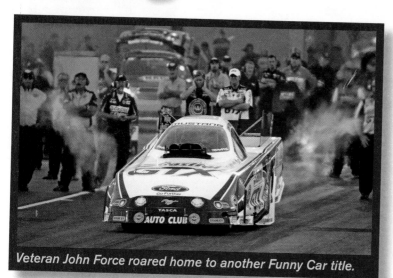

Veteran John Force roared home to another Funny Car title.

championship at that same track, Auto Club Raceway in Pomona, Calif. It was his seventh win of the season and earned him enough points to win the season title. "When all your dreams come true and you're part of something special, you're almost at a loss for words," he said. "It's a crazy feeling to win at this track where I grew up." Shawn won his first national drag-racing title when he was just 14 in the junior division.

FUNNY CAR: It was a family affair in the NHRA Funny Car division in 2013. It was no surprise to find **John Force** at the top when the dust settled. He won his record 16th season championship in the high-speed, high-risk sport. At 64 years old, he shows no signs of slowing down and retiring. "We've won the championship and we're glad to have done so, man, we're having fun. . . . I don't want to end my career at 16. I want to end it at 17 at least." The big news was the name of the driver he beat to clinch the title: his daughter **Courtney Force**!

TOP FUEL: When he was a kid, **Shawn Langdon** followed his dad, **Chad**, to the track near their house in Southern California when Chad was a pro racer. Shawn proved that home cooking suited him in 2013 as he won the Top Fuel

PRO STOCK: The 2013 season marked a real comeback for **Jeg Coughlin**. Though he had four season championships in hand, in 2012, he and his entire team struggled. They did not win a single race and plunged in the points standings. That all turned around in 2013, however, as he won four races, finished second in four others, and secured his fifth overall title on the final weekend of the season.

PRO STOCK MOTORCYCLE: Just like the Force family, the Smith family just loves to race. **Matt Smith** does his driving on motorcycles. He was fast and good enough to win his second Pro Stock Motorcycle title in 2013. These bikes really move: Smith topped 190 miles per hour in his winning race! Plus, Matt's dad, **Rickie**, won a season title in a lower-division car racing series called Pro Mod!

Mr. Motorcycle

Like **Sebastian Vettel** in Formula 1 (see page 142), **Ryan Villopoto** was "the man" in motorcycle racing in 2014. After capturing the AMA Supercross title in early 2013, he moved to the AMA Motocross series. He won five races to take a solid lead and just needed a victory in the second-to-last race of the summer in Utah to clinch it. After winning the "holeshot" (first rider to the first turn at the start), Villopoto held off rival **Ryan Dungey** at the end of the race for the victory. That gave him enough points to clinch the season title, his second ever.

Then Villopoto turned his attention to the shorter, tighter 2014 AMA Supercross series. He picked up where he had left off in Motocross by winning a series-high seven races, including the final in Las Vegas. That gave him his second straight season championship (and he has won three of the last four). He really turned it on in the second half of the season. After nine races, he had two wins. Then Villopoto won five of the next eight races, including the season's final four events. He became the second rider ever to win four straight Supercross championships.

Villopoto (No. 1) was out in front here and for the whole season!

2013 Indy Car

Scott **Dixon** didn't win the final race of the 2013 IndyCar season . . . but he did win the overall title. The driver from New Zealand captured his third IndyCar championship and first since 2008. The title was also the tenth for the Target Chip Ganassi team since 1990.

It was sweet revenge after a disaster to end the 2012 season. Coming into the last race of that year, he had the title in hand, but a final-race crash ruined his chances. This time, the racing shoe was on the other foot.

Dixon actually led the points chart early in 2013. However, Brazil's **Helio Castroneves** put on a big charge in the summer, including a win at Texas. Dixon was back in eighth place following the Indy 500. Then Dixon won three races

Scott Dixon kisses the IndyCar championship trophy.

2013 IZOD INDYCAR SERIES FINAL STANDINGS

PLACE/DRIVER	POINTS
1. Scott Dixon	577
2. Hélio Castroneves	550
3. Simon Pagenaud	508
4. Will Power	498
5. Marco Andretti	484
6. Justin Wilson	472
7. Ryan Hunter-Reay	469
8. James Hinchcliffe	449
9. Charlie Kimball	427
10. Dario Franchitti	418

in a row in July (Pocono, and both races in Toronto) to slice into the Brazilian's lead.

Castroneves was 49 points up heading into a two-race day at Houston. Dixon won the first of those races, while Castroneves's car stalled. In the second race of the day, Castroneves's car again did not work well. Dixon finished second. That reversal of fortune left Dixon on top.

In the final race of the season in California, Castroneves had to win to have a chance to move back on top, but he couldn't do it. Dixon finished fifth with enough points to drive home the overall winner.

Rising star **Simon Pagenaud** of France finished third. Even though **Will Power** won the final two races of the season, that was not enough to overcome earlier bad finishes. Dixon's fellow New Zealander finished in fourth. **Marco Andretti** (fifth) was the highest-finishing American driver.

2014 INDY 500

American drivers did not do that well in IndyCar in 2013 (see standings box). But one U.S. driver did capture the biggest race of the year—the Indianapolis 500. **Ryan Hunter-Reay** won the race by 0.06 seconds, the second-closest finish in the 103-year history of the storied race. Hunter-Reay made a dramatic pass on the final lap to overtake **Helio Castroneves** and slide over the finish line just a nose ahead.

GEARS AND WHEELS: INDYCAR

✳ In 2013, four drivers each won their first IndyCar race. That sort of rise in talent means good things for competition in the years ahead. The four first-timers: **James Hinchcliffe**, **Takuma Sato**, **Simon Pagenaud**, and **Charlie Kimball**.

✳ No one earned the million-dollar bonus for the Indy Triple Crown. Maybe next year!

✳ **Will Power** got off to a hot start in 2014. He won the season-opening race in Florida, then was in the top 10 in the next seven events.

Major Champions

OF THE 2000s

TOP FUEL DRAGSTERS

YEAR	DRIVER
2013	Shawn Langdon
2012	Antron Brown
2011	Del Worsham
2010	Larry Dixon
2009	Tony Schumacher
2008	Tony Schumacher
2007	Tony Schumacher
2006	Tony Schumacher
2005	Tony Schumacher
2004	Tony Schumacher
2003	Larry Dixon
2002	Larry Dixon
2001	Kenny Bernstein

FUNNY CARS

YEAR	DRIVER
2013	John Force
2012	Jack Beckham
2011	Matt Hagan
2010	John Force
2009	Robert Hight
2008	Cruz Pedregon
2007	Tony Pedregon
2006	John Force
2005	Gary Scelzi
2004	John Force
2003	Tony Pedregon
2002	John Force
2001	John Force

PRO STOCK CARS

YEAR	DRIVER
2013	Jeg Coughlin Jr.
2012	Allen Johnson
2011	Jason Line
2010	Greg Anderson
2009	Mike Edwards
2008	Jeg Coughlin Jr.
2007	Jeg Coughlin Jr.
2006	Jason Line
2005	Greg Anderson
2004	Greg Anderson
2003	Greg Anderson
2002	Jeg Coughlin Jr.
2001	Warren Johnson

FORMULA ONE

YEAR	DRIVER
2013	Sebastian Vettel
2012	Sebastian Vettel
2011	Sebastian Vettel
2010	Sebastian Vettel
2009	Jenson Button
2008	Lewis Hamilton
2007	Kimi Räikkönen
2006	Fernando Alonso
2005	Fernando Alonso
2004	Michael Schumacher
2003	Michael Schumacher
2002	Michael Schumacher
2001	Michael Schumacher

INDYCAR SERIES

YEAR	DRIVER
2013	Scott Dixon
2012	Ryan Hunter-Reay
2011	Dario Franchitti
2010	Dario Franchitti
2009	Dario Franchitti
2008	Scott Dixon
2007	Dario Franchitti
2006	Sam Hornish Jr. and Dan Wheldon (tie)
2005	Dan Wheldon
2004	Tony Kanaan
2003	Scott Dixon
2002	Sam Hornish Jr.
2001	Sam Hornish Jr.

AMA SUPERCROSS

YEAR	DRIVER
2014	Ryan Villopoto
2013	Ryan Villopoto
2012	Ryan Dungey
2011	Ryan Villopoto
2010	Ryan Dungey
2009	James Stewart Jr.
2008	Chad Reed
2007	James Stewart Jr.
2006	Ricky Carmichael
2005	Ricky Carmichael
2004	Chad Reed
2003	Ricky Carmichael
2002	Ricky Carmichael
2001	Ricky Carmichael

AMA MOTOCROSS

YEAR	RIDER (MOTOCROSS)	RIDER (LITES)
2013	Ryan Villopoto	Eli Tomac
2012	Ryan Dungey	Blake Baggett
2011	Ryan Villopoto	Dean Wilson
2010	Ryan Dungey	Trey Canard
2009	Chad Reed	Ryan Dungey
2008	James Stewart Jr.	Ryan Villopoto
2007	Grant Langston	Ryan Villopoto
2006	Ricky Carmichael	Ryan Villopoto
2005	Ricky Carmichael	Ivan Tedesco
2004	Ricky Carmichael	James Stewart Jr.
2003	Ricky Carmichael	Grant Langston
2002	Ricky Carmichael	James Stewart Jr.
2001	Ricky Carmichael	Mike Brown

ACTION SPORTS

A LONG WAY DOWN

Afraid of heights? Then this is definitely not the sport for you. Brave and daring and talented, cliff divers leap from enormous heights . . . and do spins and twists on the way down! Then they smack into the water. Wow! The platforms are more than 90 feet (28 meters) above the water. As thrilled fans watch from far below, the divers plummet down. In 2014, Britain's Gary Hunt was one of the top divers in the worldwide Red Bull series. Women also dove for the first time and American Rachelle Simpson led the pack.

Summer X Games

Bestwick's the Best!

The old man's still got it! For the ninth time in a row, extending his X Games record, **Jamie Bestwick** soared to victory in BMX Vert. Throwing down tricks like the 540 one-foot seatgrab combo, Bestwick showed that age equals experience in this high-flying sport. Bestwick got his golden start way back in 1996; this year's medal gives him a lucky 13 all-time in X Games events.

Flying Kid!

In the skateboard big air event, most experts pegged **Bob Burnquist** of Brazil to win again. He's been a champion in this sport for a decade. But this time around, **Tom Schaar**, 14 years old, soared above everyone to win the gold. In the event, skaters descend a nearly vertical ramp more than 30 feet above the arena floor. After flying across two ramps, they then rocket straight up. Whoever flies highest and scores best wins. This year, it was the kid, who put up a score of 89 in the third run that no one could top.

The Perfect Name

With a name like **Scott Speed**, it's no surprise that he's a racing champion. Speed has already been a driver on the NASCAR and Formula 1 circuits. He took up rally driving and has dominated there. At the X Games in Austin, Speed sped to the lead in both heats of the RallyCross. In the final, he led all 10 laps and roared away with his second straight gold medal.

SKATE KING

Nyjah Huston had the best run in the first round of skateboard street. Then in the second run, he nailed a nollie 270 lip slide on the last rail and nailed down the championship. It was the young star's fifth X Games medal in skateboarding.

Rough and Tumble

Americans dominated at the X Games, winning all but five of the 18 gold medals. The only out-of-towner to win a Moto X medal was **Tadeusz Blazusiak** of Poland. He navigated the rocky, bumpy, dusty, hilly course faster than anyone else in Moto X Enduro.

2014 SUMMER X GAMES CHAMPS

BMX

VERT	**Jamie Bestwick**
FREESTYLE STREET	**Garrett Reynolds**
DIRT	**Kyle Braddock**
FREESTYLE BIG AIR	**Colton Satterfield**

MOTO X

M ENDURO	**Tadeusz Blazusiak**
W ENDURO	**Kacey Martinez**
BEST WHIP	**Tom Parsons**
STEP UP	**Ronnie Renner**
SPEED & STYLE	**Mike Mason**

RALLYING

LITES	**Mitchell DeJong**
RALLYCROSS	**Scott Speed**
SUPER TRUCKS	**Apdaly Lopez**

SKATEBOARDING

FREESTYLE VERT	**Jimmy Wilkins**
BIG AIR	**Tom Schaar**
PARK	**Pedro Barros**
STREET AMATEURS	**Tyson Bowerbank**
W STREET	**Lacey Baker**
M STREET	**Nyjah Huston**

Tadeusz Blazusiak (111) outmuscled the competition in Moto X Enduro.

Winter X Games

Colten Moore thrilled friends and family by winning while honoring his late brother.

It was lucky 13 in 2014 for the Winter X Games. The annual gathering of the most high-flying, snow-churning winter action stars returned to Aspen, Colorado, for the 13th time. Here are some of the highlights of more than a week of awesomeness.

One for Bro

In 2013, **Caleb Moore** was killed while attempting a trick in snowmobile freestyle. In 2014, his brother **Colten** thrilled fans by capturing a gold medal in the same event. "This one is for Caleb," he said before his final ride. The brothers' parents were on hand to cheer for Colton . . . and remember Caleb.

The X Games Queen

It was nothing new, but it was something special. **Kelly Clark** won her fourth straight snowboard superpipe event, giving her 12 X Games medals, more than any other female competitor. It was also the 70th victory in any competition for Clark. Finishing second behind Clark was probable future X Games champ **Chloe Kim**, who was only 13 when she earned silver. She was only 0.67 points behind the champion, while trailing her by 18 in the years department!

(Lucky 7) x 3

Okay, no fair throwing math at you. What that means is that a pair of X Games athletes each won their seventh gold medals during the Aspen event. First, in snowmobile snocross, **Tucker Hibbert** became the first person ever to win seven straight golds. He roared across the finish line (or should we say over the finish line, as he was airborne at the time!) 14 seconds ahead of **Koby Kamm**.

In Snowboarder X, **Nate Holland** got his seventh gold as well, though not in a row. His event is a rock-and-roll ride combining cross-country and jumping while riding snowboards.

In the men's snowboard superpipe event, there was a chance for yet another seven-peat. However, superstar **Shaun White**, who had already won the event six times, skipped the X Games to prepare for the Winter Olympics in Sochi (page 54). So **Danny Davis** earned his first gold medal . . . in his seventh try!

Flying superstar! Kelly Clark soared to her seventh gold.

Double Gold

In the bird world, parrots are known for repeating what people say to them. In the X Games, **Max Parrot** is now known for repeating gold medals! He was the only male athlete to win a pair of golds, capturing snowboard big air and snowboard slopestyle.

❝Whenever I decide to leave, it's going to be in good hands.❞

— KELLY CLARK ON
KNOWING THAT YOUNG SNOWBOARDERS
ARE READY TO CARRY ON HER SUCCESS

2014 WINTER X GAMES CHAMPS

SNOWMOBILE FREESTYLE	**Colten MOORE**	SNOWMOBILE LONG JUMP	**Levi LAVALLEE**
M SNOWBOARDER X	**Nate HOLLAND**	SKI BIG AIR	**Henrik HARLAUT**
W SNOWBOARDER X	**Lindsey JACOBELLIS**	SKI SLOPESTYLE	**Nick GOEPPER**
W SKI SUPERPIPE	**Maddie BOWMAN**	SNOCROSS ADAPTIVE	**Mike SCHULTZ**
M SKI SUPERPIPE	**David WISE**	W SKI SLOPESTYLE	**Kaya TURSKI**
M SNOWBOARD BIG AIR	**Max PARROT**	SNOWMOBILE SNOWCROSS	**Tucker HIBBERT**
M SNOWBOARD SLOPESTYLE	**Max PARROT**	M SNOWBOARD SUPERPIPE	**Danny DAVIS**
W SNOWBOARD SLOPESTYLE	**Silje NORENDAL**	W SNOWBOARD SUPERPIPE	**Kelly CLARK**

Action Notes

Surfing Champion 2013

Slow and steady proved to be the winning formula for surfer **Mick Fanning**. The Australian only won one event on the Association of Surfing Professionals (ASP) Tour, but he finished third or better five other times. That racked up enough points to give him his third career ASP crown. The race actually came down to the final heats in the last event of the summer. Fanning caught a huge wave off Oahu's North Shore and rode it to the winning points.

BIG WAVES!

Riding waves that towered as much as 50 feet high, bold surfers once again took the Mavericks' challenge. The annual event off Northern California only happens when the surf gets big enough. In 2014, the waves rose in January, and **Grant Baker** rose above the competition to win his second Mavericks' big-wave event.

Mick Fanning hits the top of a wave on his way to another ASP world championship.

Sheckler: Three wins in a row!

Longest Triathlon

Triathletes are already the world's most versatile endurance athletes. But in 2014, **Norma Bastidas** put even those amazing athletes in the dust. She completed the longest triathlon ever, a grueling trek across that took her 65 days. First, she struggled through a 95-mile swim in the Caribbean. The longest leg came next, 2,932 miles on a bike, from Mexico into the southern United States. Then she left Georgia on a 735-mile run that ended in Washington, DC. The 46-year-old did the record "tri" to call attention to the worldwide problem of violence against women.

Dew Tour Report

❋ A pair of action-sports championships provided thrills for fans on either side of the country. In June, Ocean City, Maryland, was home to the Beach Championships. **Bucky Lasek** won the Beach Bowl skateboarding event, edging out 14-year-old **Tom Schaar**. In the BMX Vert event, **Jamie Bestwick** just kept flying. He won his tenth straight title in that high-flying event.

❋ In August, the tour headed west to Portland, Oregon. **Ryan Sheckler** won the skate streetstyle for the third straight year. "When you are a little kid all you want to do is bomb hills," he said afterward. "So to have a downhill contest with a bunch of gnarly ramps on it just spoke to me. I love skating this event!" The BMX riders got their chance on the streets of Portland, too, and **Dennis Enarson** came out the winner in Streetstyle.

Try, Try, Try, and Try Again

That's the code endurance swimmer **Diana Nyad** lives by. Four times, she had tried to swim from Florida to Cuba without using a protective shark cage. Four times she had to get out of the water, exhausted. In 2013, she tried again . . . and this time she made it! The 64-year-old athlete needed 53 hours to swim the 103 miles. Her mouth and lips swelled from the saltwater and she had to eat and drink while she swam, but she kept going. She did have a boat alongside to help protect her, but the swimming was all her. Turned out it was worth another try!

GOLF

NO. 1
Thanks to two Major championships and solid success all season, Rory McIlroy took over the top spot in the World Golf Rankings. The way he's playing, it might be a while before he loses it!

McMagic!

Finally, a year in which the biggest news in golf was not **Tiger Woods**! Tiger was still out there, but back problems plagued him in 2014. The spotlight shone instead on another golfer who was, like Tiger before him, racking up majors at a very young age. **Rory McIlroy** has been a rising star for several years, but in 2014, he really made a big leap forward into the ranks of the all-time greats.

The Masters Championship at Augusta National is always the highlight of the golf year. Its many traditions, like the winner's green jacket, are a steady light in an ever-changing sports scene. In 2014, the winner actually was putting on his second green jacket. **Bubba Watson** had won in 2012, so he knew what to do when he trailed early in the final round. The long-drive expert set himself up for key birdies at the turn and then held off several other golfers with a final-round 69.

At the US Open, Germany's **Martin Kaymer** got off to a record-setting start. His total of 130 after the first two rounds was the lowest in Open history. He wound up trouncing the field, winning by eight shots over the best golfers in the world.

McIlroy, meanwhile, had been mostly absent from the first two Majors. But he heated up in the summer. At the British Open, McIlroy was romping almost as well as Kaymer had. The young star from Northern Ireland held a six-shot lead as play began on the final day. A determined **Sergio Garcia**, however, charged after him. McIlroy led by only two shots after the 13th hole. However, he played flawless golf the rest of the way. His total was only two shots shy of the all-time British Open record set by Woods in 2000. It was McIlroy's first British Open victory, leaving him one short of the "career Grand Slam." He has previously won a US Open and a PGA Championship.

In August, he added another gem to that crown. But he had to work overtime to get it done. At the PGA Championship, McIlroy started the day in the lead, but **Phil Mickelson**, **Henrik Stenson**, and **Rickie Fowler** sent him as low as fourth. But McIlroy stayed steady. Finally, he overtook Mickelson on the 10th hole. As the light was dimming over the course in Kentucky, the pair finished just in time. McIlroy ended just one shot ahead of "Lefty," but that was enough to give him four Majors at the age of 25. Only Woods and the great **Jack Nicklaus** had won as many so young.

2014 MEN'S MAJORS

THE MASTERS
Bubba Watson

THE US OPEN
Martin Kaymer

THE BRITISH OPEN
Rory McIlroy

THE PGA CHAMPIONSHIP
Rory McIlroy

Presidents Cup

The most famous international golf team event is the Ryder Cup, between the United States and golfers from Europe. But golf is played around the world, not just Europe. So in 1994, the Presidents Cup was created to pit an American team against golfers from everywhere else! The 2013 event was held in Ohio. Thanks to the home-course advantage, the first two days saw a big show of support from US fans, but a loud group of Aussie supporters brought splashes of color to the stands. After two days, the US held a slim 1-point lead but the rain slowed down the action.

On Saturday, Tiger Woods and Matt Kuchar, who won all three of their matches, added a key four-ball victory on Saturday. That was one of four big wins that put the US team in charge when play was suspended due to darkness on Saturday.

Early Sunday, the Americans romped, giving them a big lead heading into Sunday afternoon's singles. In fact, the International team trailed by nine points heading in. They needed to win 10 of 12 matches to take the Cup.

A 65-foot putt by Hunter Mahan helped him earn an early point for the US. Graham Delaet of Canada chipped in from the sand to earn a point for the Internationals. After a couple more wins by the Americans, however, the Cup-clinching point was earned by Tiger Woods. It was the third straight Presidents'

Tiger Woods clinched the Cup again!

Cup that Tiger had clinched, and the third championship for captain Fred Couples. The final score was 18.5–15.5.

The next Presidents Cup will be in the fall of 2015 in South Korea.

2013 PRESIDENTS CUP US TEAM

CAPTAIN: Fred Couples

Keegan Bradley	Phil Mickelson
Jason Dufner	Webb Simpson
Bill Haas	Brent Snedaker
Zach Johnson	Jordan Spieth
Matt Kuchar	Steve Stricker
Hunter Mahan	Tiger Woods

Chip Shots

One for Them, One for Me

Matt Kuchar got it coming and going in early 2014. At the Houston Open, he made it into a playoff with Matt Jones. But then Jones buried a chip from 42 feet out to snatch the victory.

Then, just two weeks later, Kuchar got revenge . . . sort of. Trailing by four strokes heading into the final round of the RBC Heritage event in South Carolina, he got within a stroke of winning near the end. Then, on the 18th hole, tied for the lead, he chipped the ball into the cup for his own sudden victory! Turnabout was fair play, as they say.

Rising Stars?

Heading into 2014, the only people who had heard of Jimmy Walker were probably his family and his caddy. After winning three times in the first half of the year and leading the PGA Tour in earnings for months, Walker was a mystery no longer. He was steady, too, finishing in the top 10 nine times in his first 23 starts. Keep an eye on him heading into a Ryder Cup season in 2015. Also, Jordan Spieth is one to watch. Though only 20, he has three top-five finishes in Majors (and a solid finish in the FedEx Cup) and helped the US win the Presidents Cup.

Jordan Spieth is one of the top young players.

Another Mr. 59

Golfers aim for the low score, right? Well, the lowest score ever achieved in a PGA round is 59. It's only been done six times in more than 75 years. At the 2013 BMW Championship, Jim Furyk became the latest. He needed only 23 putts and finished with a pair of birdies to reach the magic mark. The bad news came two days later when he finished third in the tournament!

Big Money!

Tiger Woods did not have a very good 2014 (see page 159) but he had a pretty excellent 2013! He won five times and made the finals of the FedEx Cup. Golfers earn points all season long in the Cup race. The top finishers play off in a three-match series at the end of the PGA season with millions of dollars in bonus money on the line.

However, Woods did not end up the big winner in that competition.

Henrik Stenson (right) of Sweden won the Tour Championship event and with it the FedEx Cup . . . which came with a stunning $10 million bonus! He became the first player from Europe to win the big event and the big payday. Woods managed only a 22nd-place finish in the final tournament. But don't worry too much about him: Tiger still ended up as the leading money-winner of the year (not including bonuses) and also had the lowest scoring average.

Stenson's big cup can hold his winnings.

OTHER WINNERS

The PGA Tour has other groups of players competing for a title.

Champions Tour Players fifty and over take part in a series of tournaments with just as much competitive fire as they had in their younger days . . . but with perhaps shorter drives! In 2013, **Kenny Perry** won the most tournaments, with three, but it was German ace Bernhard Langer who won the all-important money title. It was the second straight year he ended on top of the 50-plus crowd.

Web.com Tour Younger golfers aiming at the PGA Tour can earn a big step up on this second-level tour. The top 25 finishers of the season's combined events automatically got PGA Tour cards. **Michael Putnam** won the most money heading into the season-ending "Final Four." **Chasson Headley** won the Web.com Tour Championship. Both had their PGA dreams come true.

LPGA Update

Since she was only about 10 years old, **Michelle Wie** has been one of the most famous golfers in the world, male or female. She played in a national tournament that year and then won the Hawaii state championship when she was just 13. A star at a young age, she even played in a men's PGA tournament. But her early promise had not really matched the hype . . . until 2014. In April, she broke a 79-match winless streak with a tournament victory in her home state of Hawaii. Then in July, she earned her first Major championship. With a clutch birdie on the 17th hole of the US Women's Open, Wie clinched the victory and got a Major monkey off her back.

"Michelle winning was a massive boost for the women's game," said English player **Laura Davies**. "She's box office. She's our **Tiger** [**Woods**], basically."

Wie's win was part of a great run by American women golfers on the year. In recent seasons, golfers from Asia have dominated the LPGA, but US athletes got back in the hunt in

Michelle Wie

LPGA MAJOR WINNERS

KRAFT NABISCO CHAMPIONSHIP
Lexi Thompson

US WOMEN'S OPEN
Michelle Wie

WOMEN'S BRITISH OPEN
Mo Martin

WEGMAN'S LPGA CHAMPIONSHIP
Inbee Park

EVIAN CHAMPIONSHIP
Hyo-Joo Kim

2014. Americans won the first four of the Major tournaments (see box), including Wie's Open title. Meanwhile, **Inbee Park** of Korea, the dominant player in 2013, did win her second straight LPGA Championship.

Other Season Highlights:

✳ American star **Stacy Lewis** regained the world Number 1 ranking in June.

✳ Through August, five different golfers each won two tournaments.

✳ The 11 wins by American golfers through early August was the most in any single season in the 2000s.

The Majors

In golf, some tournaments are known as the Majors. They're the four most important events of the year on either the men's or the women's pro tours. **Tiger Woods** has the most career wins in Majors among current golfers. **Annika Sörenstam** retired in 2010 with the most among recent LPGA players.

MEN'S

	MASTERS	US OPEN	BRITISH OPEN	PGA CHAMP.	TOTAL
Jack **NICKLAUS**	6	4	3	5	18
Tiger **WOODS**	4	3	3	4	14
Walter **HAGEN**	0	2	4	5	11
Ben **HOGAN**	2	4	1	2	9
Gary **PLAYER**	3	1	3	2	9
Tom **WATSON**	2	1	5	0	8
Arnold **PALMER**	4	1	2	0	7
Gene **SARAZEN**	1	2	1	3	7
Sam **SNEAD**	3	0	1	3	7
Harry **VARDON**	0	1	6	0	7

PRESIDENTS CUP
The past winners of the Presidents Cup

2013: UNITED STATES

2011: UNITED STATES

2009: UNITED STATES

2007: UNITED STATES

2005: UNITED STATES

2003: UNITED STATES

2000: UNITED STATES

1996: UNITED STATES

1994: UNITED STATES

1998: INTERNATIONAL TEAM

WOMEN'S

	LPGA	USO	BO	NAB	MAUR	TH	WES	TOTAL
Patty **BERG**	0	1	x	x	x	7	7	15
Mickey **WRIGHT**	4	4	x	x	x	2	3	13
Louise **SUGGS**	1	2	x	x	x	4	4	11
Annika **SÖRENSTAM**	3	3	1	3	x	x	x	10
Babe **ZAHARIAS**	x	3	x	x	x	3	4	10
Betsy **RAWLS**	2	4	x	x	x	x	2	8
Juli **INKSTER**	2	2	x	2	1	x	x	7
Karrie **WEBB**	1	2	1	2	1	x	x	7

KEY: LPGA = LPGA Championship, USO = US Open, BO = British Open, NAB = Nabisco Championship, MAUR = du Maurier (1979–2000), TH = Titleholders (1937–1972), WES = Western Open (1937–1967)

PGA TOUR CAREER EARNINGS*

1. Tiger Woods — $109,612,414
2. Phil Mickelson — $75,260,366
3. Vijay Singh — $68,520,532
4. Jim Furyk — $60,559,833
5. Ernie Els — $47,298,592
6. Davis Love III — $42,796,746
7. Steve Stricker — $40,674,840
8. David Toms — $40,231,394
9. Sergio Garcia — $37,202,413
10. Adam Scott — $36,589,758

LPGA TOUR CAREER EARNINGS*

1. Annika Sörenstam — $22,573,192
2. Karrie Webb — $18,821,492
3. Cristie Kerr — $15,816,446
4. Lorena Ochoa — $14,863,331
5. Juli Inkster — $13,681,019

*Through July 2014

ADAM SCOTT

Check out that list of big money winners on the PGA Tour. That's a lot of green for hitting a ball to the greens! In 2014, a new player cracked that top 10. Australia's Adam Scott pocketed $1.5 million for a high finish in the FedEx Cup, and added another $3 million-plus through July. He's been a steady star since joining the PGA Tour in 2000. The biggest highlight of his career was winning the 2013 Masters Tournament. With all that money, he'll have no problem flying back from Australia to Georgia every spring to play the Masters!

TENNIS

NINE FOR NADAL
Spanish star Rafael Nadal won his record ninth French Open in 2014. That gave him 14 Grand Slam tournament wins, tied for second all-time behind Swiss star Roger Federer.

Men's Tennis

There are no ties in tennis, but **Novak Djokovic** and **Rafael Nadal** are proving to be pretty close to one. The perennial superstars have dominated tennis in the past few years, taking turns winning Grand Slams and holding the Number 1 spot. In 2014, it was no different. Through August, each had won three tournaments and each had captured one Grand Slam championship. They were ranked 1-2 in the world, with nearly twice as many points as the Number 3 player, the up-and-coming **Stan Wawrinka**. But he still has a long way to go to catch the dynamic duo of tennis.

Wawrinka did break the logjam at the Australian Open. Wawrinka beat Rafael Nadal in an upset to win his first Grand Slam event. True, Nadal played with an injured back. "I'll take it," Wawrinka said. It was only the second Grand Slam win by any player except Nadal, Djokovic, **Roger Federer**, or **Andy Murray** in the past eight years. Wawrinka moved to No. 3 in the world with his big win.

Things got back to normal at the French Open. Nadal won his all-time record ninth

This is the tournament I grew up dreaming about winning. So it never gets boring winning it again. This was the best Grand Slam final I have ever played in.

— 2014 WIMBLEDON CHAMPION NOVAK DJOKOVIC

title in Paris, and his fifth in a row. "For me," Nadal said, "playing here in Roland Garros is just unforgettable, forever." It's pretty forgettable for anyone who has to play him. His serve-and-volley game is perfect for the clay courts of this event.

Djokovic had been on a Grand Slam mini-drought. He won the 2013 Australian Open, but then lost a pair of Grand Slam finals or didn't even make the finals of others. At Wimbledon in 2014, however, he got back on the winning track. He also took over the No. 1 ranking from Nadal, as they played their own version of digital Ping-Pong back and forth in the standings. To win his second Wimbledon (the first was back in 2011), he had to dig deep to defeat **Roger Federer** of Switzerland, the all-time leader with 17 Grand Slams. It took Djokovic nearly four hours and five full sets to beat Federer in a match called one of the best Wimbledon finals in recent years.

At the US Open, Japan's **Kei Nishikori** became the first Asian player ever to reach a Grand Slamp final after upsetting Djokovic. He faced **Marin Cilic**, a surprise winner over Federer. Cilic won in straight sets to capture his first Grand Slam title.

2014 MEN'S GRAND SLAMS

AUSTRALIAN OPEN	**Stan Wawrinka**
FRENCH OPEN	**Rafael Nadal**
WIMBLEDON	**Novak Djokovic**
US OPEN	**Marin Cilic**

Women's Tennis

Veteran **Li Na** capped off her fine career with her second Grand Slam title and first Aussie championship. At 32, she became the oldest woman to win "Down Under" since 1968. She also erased the memory of losing in the finals in this event in 2013 after turning an ankle and falling on her head. In fact, she almost repeated that performance, but saved a match point against a tough opponent in **Dominika Cibulkova**. Meanwhile, **Eugenie Bouchard** was making history of her own. She became the first Canadian player to reach the semis of this historic tournament.

At the French Open, the competition was actually that–open. For the first time since "open" tennis began in 1968, none of the top three seeds in the women's tournament made it to the semifinals. After a series of upsets sent the top players packing, it fell to another veteran to claim the title. Russian star **Maria Sharapova**, 27 and in her 13th year of pro tennis, rallied to win her second French Open (she also won in 2012).

When Wimbledon began, naturally everyone looked to **Serena Williams**, eyeing her sixth championship in England. However, Williams bowed out early, and sneaking up through the bracket was a player some thought might have hit her only jackpot while winning Wimbledon in 2011. But **Petra Kvitova** showed she was more than a one-hit wonder. She beat the fast-rising Bouchard in the final, winning in straight sets and losing only three games.

At the US Open, Williams got her game back. In winning her sixth Open, she didn't lose a set, dominating a string of opponents. The win solidified her role as the top women's player in the world.

2014 WOMEN'S GRAND SLAMS	
AUSTRALIAN OPEN	**Li Na**
FRENCH OPEN	**Maria Sharapova**
WIMBLEDON	**Petra Kvitova**
US OPEN	**Serena Williams**

Kvitova, like Djokovic, made it a pair of Wimbledons in 2014.

Tennis Notes

A Grand for Roger ▶▶▶

The Masters 1000 series of tournaments is the top level of pro tennis events. In 2014, **Roger Federer** became the first player ever to win 300 matches in those top events. He won his first way back in 2000 and reached No. 300 with a victory at the ATP event in Cincinnati in August.

Serena's Swoon

During the 2014 Wimbledon doubles competition, **Serena Williams** was either super brave or super crazy. She and her sister **Venus** were playing together, as they always do. But the match was delayed while Serena was looked at by a doctor. She started the match, but was wiped out. Her once-mighty serves didn't even reach the net. The sisters lost the first three games of the match. After barely hitting the ball, Serena had to leave the court. It turned out that she had a virus, but it was a weird scene until she finally gave in.

Czech Mates

The Davis Cup is an annual, year-long tournament that pits top tennis countries against each other. Teams play two doubles and three singles matches. Win and play on; lose and you're done. In 2013, the Czech Republic repeated as champions, defeating Serbia 3–2 in Serbia's capital of Belgrade. And Serbia boasted the No. 1 player, **Novak Djokovic**, but the Czechs had more depth. **Radek Stepanek** became only the third player ever to clinch the Cup in the fifth game in back-to-back years.

Where Are We?

While **Serena Williams** is number one among women, the highest-ranked American male player is **John Isner** at 14th. There was only one other American in the top 50!

Grand Slams

ALL-TIME GRAND SLAM CHAMPIONSHIPS (MEN)

	AUS. OPEN	FRENCH OPEN	WIMBLEDON	US OPEN	TOTAL
Roger **FEDERER**	4	1	7	5	**17**
Pete **SAMPRAS**	2	0	7	5	**14**
Rafael **NADAL**	1	9	2	2	**14**
Roy **EMERSON**	6	2	2	2	**12**
Björn **BORG**	0	6	5	0	**11**
Rod **LAVER**	3	2	4	2	**11**
Bill **TILDEN**	0	0	3	7	**10**
Jimmy **CONNORS**	1	0	2	5	**8**
Ivan **LENDL**	2	3	0	3	**8**
Fred **PERRY**	1	1	3	3	**8**
Ken **ROSEWALL**	4	2	0	2	**8**
Andre **AGASSI**	4	1	1	2	**8**

PETE SAMPRAS Until Roger Federer

overtook him in 2012, Sampras was the all-time Grand Slam champ. He did most of his damage at Wimbledon, where he set a record with seven championships (Federer later tied that mark), while also winning five US Opens. A tall, powerful, California native, Sampras excelled in the serve-and-volley game. His long arms made him a force at the net, able to slam down nearly any passing shot, but with the touch to make nasty drop shots, too. The only hole in his record was a lack of French Open titles, but the slower clay was not his best surface. That did not stop him from being the world No. 1 for six straight years through 1998.

ALL-TIME GRAND SLAM CHAMPIONSHIPS (WOMEN)

	AUS.	FRENCH	WIMBLEDON	US	TOTAL
Margaret Smith **COURT**	11	5	3	5	**24**
Steffi **GRAF**	4	6	7	5	**22**
Helen Wills **MOODY**	0	4	8	7	**19**
Chris **EVERT**	2	7	3	6	**18**
Martina **NAVRATILOVA**	3	2	9	4	**18**
Serena **WILLIAMS**	5	2	5	6	**18**
Billie Jean **KING**	1	1	6	4	**12**
Maureen **CONNOLLY**	1	2	3	3	**9**
Monica **SELES**	4	3	0	2	**9**
Suzanne **LENGLEN**	0	2*	6	0	**8**
Molla Bjurstedt **MALLORY**	0	0	0	8	**8**

*Also won 4 French titles before 1925; in those years, the tournament was open only to French nationals.

CAREER GRAND SLAMS

(Year represents fourth win of four Grand Slam events. Players with an * also won an Olympic gold medal.)

Maria SHARAPOVA (2012)

Serena WILLIAMS* (2003)

Steffi GRAF* (1988)

Martina NAVRATILOVA (1983)

Chris EVERT (1982)

Billie Jean KING (1972)

Margaret SMITH COURT (1963)

Shirley Fry IRVIN (1957)

Maureen CONNOLLY (1953)

Doris HART (1954)

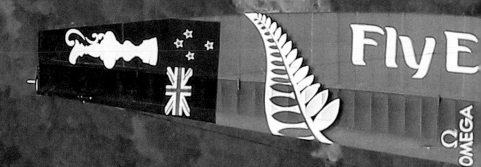

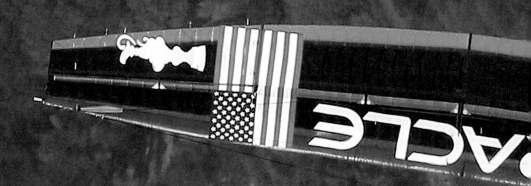

WHAT A FINISH!
In the America's Cup, the Team USA Oracle and the Team New Zealand boats were each 72-foot long catamarans with high-tech solid sails that towered more than 13 stories above the choppy water. They could go as fast as 50 miles an hour. Special wings even let them zip over the water almost like hovercraft! But as cool as that all is . . . it was the racing that really made news. Turn the page to find out why!

America's Cup

When you think of exciting sports, you don't normally think of yacht racing. There's no ball, for one thing, and all the races are held way out on the water. And the rules are strange and some days they can't race because there's not enough wind (or too much!). But in 2013, American sports fans saw something really amazing.

The America's Cup sailboat races have been held regularly since 1851. Americans dominated the race for more than a century, but international challengers have won several times in recent decades. Heading into 2013, an American team owned the Cup and chose San Francisco Bay as the site of the finals. They faced a team from New Zealand that had emerged from a group of challengers.

In the finals, the teams would race over more than two weeks. The first team to win nine races would be the champ. For a while, it looked like they wouldn't need two weeks. New Zealand just clobbered the American team. They won race after race, eventually leading 8–1.

But then a comeback started. For more than a week, the Americans chipped away at the lead. Finally, amazingly, they tied it at

Team USA skipper (or captain) Jimmy Spithill shows off the fancy silver Cup his team had just won in dramatic fashion.

8 wins apiece. That set up a showdown that was watched by millions of Americans who had become instant sailing fans thanks to the ongoing drama.

In the deciding race, the Americans continued to have more speed than the New Zealanders. About halfway through, they edged ahead and maintained that lead to the end. It was one of the greatest comebacks in American sports history (though for New Zealand, one of the biggest disappointments). The America's Cup stayed where it belonged . . . in America!

$450,000,000

That's how much sailing experts estimate that the US team spent on researching and building its boat as well as putting on the entire America's Cup.

Winter Sports
Skiin' and Skatin'!

World Cup Skiing

With **Lindsey Vonn** out with a knee injury, the field was wide open for the women's World Cup skiing championship. Austria's **Anna Fenniger** took advantage, using her downhill skills to pack up enough points to win her first world title. Fenninger was the season champ in the giant slalom and finished second in downhill and Super-G. All three types of skiing call for daring and speed, and she came through as the Cup races throughout Europe, the US, and Canada. American Olympic hero **Mikaela Shiffrin** continued her success, winning the season title in her specialty, the slalom.

On the men's side, it was business as usual. **Marcel Hirscher** not only gave Austria a sweep of the titles, but he became the first skier since American **Phil Mahre** in 1983 to win three straight overall championships. Hirscher won only the slalom discipline, but was second in giant slalom. He squeaked out the overall title from downhill and Super-G winner **Aksel Lund Svindal** of Norway. American **Ted Ligety** defended his world title in the giant slalom.

World Figure Skating Championships

Mao Asada of Japan is probably glad she stuck around. After she finished sixth at the Sochi Olympics, she thought about hanging up her skates. She was 23, after all, and had already won two world championships. But she came back for one more and surprised herself and many fans by winning the 2014 title, too. In the past 45 years, only two other skaters have won three world crowns. In another surprise, no US skaters finished in the top three in any of the events at the World Championships.

Another Japanese skater triumphed at the Worlds. **Yuzuru Hanyu** had already won gold at the Olympics (page 59). At the Worlds on home ice in Japan, he made it two for two. He was the first man since **Alexei Yagudin** to win both in the same year. The teenager was a surprise winner in Sochi, but was the favorite at the Worlds. He held on to win by less than a point over **Tatsuki Machida**.

Fenninger's victory was part of a World Cup sweep by Austrians.

Horseracing
Two for Three!

California Chrome won the Kentucky Derby.

California Chrome won the first two legs of the Triple Crown (the Kentucky Derby and Preakness). Fans loved watching the horse's owners, too. **Perry Martin** and **Steve Coburn** were not traditional horse-breeding experts with tons of money. They had purchased Chrome for less than $10,000. Plus, the horse's trainer, **Art Sherman**, was 77 years old. He had been training for 59 years and never had a horse even reach the Derby. As Chrome won and won, sports fans everywhere loved watching how the "little guys" were sticking it to the big money.

When Chrome won the Derby as an underdog, American fans rallied behind him. Then Chrome won the Preakness in Maryland and Triple Crown talk began. No horse has won all three legs of horseracing's most famous prize since Affirmed did it in 1978. At the final leg, the Belmont Stakes in New York, Chrome struggled over the longer distance. He gave it a good try, but finished fourth. Once again, the Triple Crown would have to wait another year.

A few years ago, the story of a racehorse out of California that few thought would succeed captured America's attention. Of course, that story happened in 1938 and it took a popular, Oscar-nominated movie to remind people about **Seabiscuit**.

In 2014, however, another horse from out West became pretty famous, too.

2014 TRIPLE CROWN RACES

RACE	RACE TRACK/SITE	WINNER/JOCKEY
KENTUCKY DERBY	CHURCHILL DOWNS/LOUISVILLE, KENTUCKY	California Chrome/Victor Espinoza
PREAKNESS	PIMLICO RACE COURSE/BALTIMORE, MARYLAND	California Chrome/Victor Espinoza
BELMONT STAKES	BELMONT PARK/ELMONT, NEW YORK	Tonality/Joel Rosario

Track & Field
2014 World Records

In a non-Olympic year, the biggest news in track and field came when people set new world records. Here are some of the most important new marks.

❉ In February, **Renaud Lavillenie** ▶▶▶ pole-vaulted 20 feet, 2.5 inches (6.16 meters) to break a record set by all-time great **Sergey Bubka** way back in 1993. Lavillenie, from France, set the mark at a meet in Ukraine.

❉ At the World Relay Championships, a pair of Kenyan quartets shattered world marks. First, the women's 4 x1,500-meter team knocked an amazing 32 seconds off the previous mark. **Mercy Cherono**, **Faith Kipyegon**, **Irene Jelagat**, and **Hellen Obiri** scorched the track in 16:33.48. drop of 32 seconds.

❉ In the same event, the Kenyan men also set a record, though not as dramatically as their countrywomen. **Collins Cheboi**, **Silas Kiplagat**, **James Magut**, and **Asbel Kiprop** lowered the record by 14 seconds.

❉ The always-powerful Jamaican sprinters added to their long record of success. But this time they did it without world-record-holder **Usain Bolt**. In the 4x200-meter relay, **Nickel Ashmeade**, **Warren Weir**, **Jermaine Brown**, and **Yohan Blake** sped through their paces in 1:18.68. That broke a record set in 1994 by a US team.

❉ Indoor racing presents special challenges. The tracks are shorter, the curves are tighter, and racers are not enjoying the fresh air. But it still takes speed and skill to win and set records. Ethiopia's **Genzebe Dibaba** set a new mark in the indoor 1,500 meters at 3:55.17.

❉ American indoor runners got a pair of world marks in 2014. At the World Indoor Championships, a quartet of speedsters set a new world record in the 4x400-meter relay. They broke a record set in 1999 by another American team. The winning team was **Kyle Clemons**, **David Verburg**, **Kind Butler III**, and **Calvin Smith**; they finished in 3:02.13.

Lacrosse
Repeat Champs!

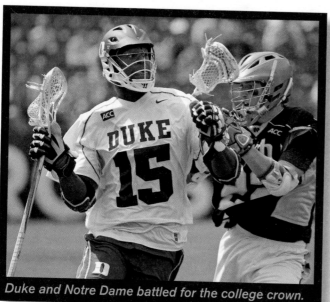
Duke and Notre Dame battled for the college crown.

NCAA

Usually, when you think of Duke University and sports, you think of its men's basketball team, which is always in the hunt for a national title. In 2013, its football team was also outstanding. Lost in the "big sports" shuffle is lacrosse. In 2014, the Blue Devils won their second-straight men's lacrosse title, and third in five seasons. To make it back to back, they had to hold off a powerful Notre Dame team.

Duke got off to a good start, allowing only one goal in the first 35 minutes. But the second-half action was fast and furious. Trailing 8-2, Notre Dame poured in the points. Duke led only 9-8 with five minutes left before closing with two late goals to clinch the 11–9 win.

National Lacrosse League

The Miami Heat could not do it in the NBA, but the Rochester Knighthawks did in the NLL. The NLL has nine teams that play an 18-game season of indoor lacrosse. In May, Rochester became the first team in NLL history to earn three straight league championships. Led by outstanding play in goal by **Matt Vinc**, Rochester beat the Calgary Roughnecks, 16–10. Forward **Dan Dawson** was named the MVP of the Finals. He had three goals in the championship, but he was one of nine different Knighthawks to score at least once. Calgary didn't have an answer for that kind of depth, nor for the netminding of Vinc.

Major League Lacrosse

The 14-game outdoor MLL season came to an exciting end in August as **Drew Smith** of the Outlaws scored the championship-clinching goal with just 56 seconds left in the final. Denver beat the Rochester Rattlers, 12–11. It was the first title in Denver team history. Denver's **John Grant Jr.** was the MVP after scoring a hat trick in the final. He won his fifth MLL championship with his third team.

Gymnastics

Fans at the US Gymnastics Championships in August were doing double-takes. After all the flips, spins, jumps, and twirls were over, the same two gymnasts from last year ended up on top.

On the women's side, **Simone Biles** made it two straight, finishing ahead of last year's runner-up **Kyla Ross**. Biles' score of 122.55 was the highest at the event since 2008! Biles won the vault and the floor exercises, while Ross captured the balance beam.

The men's champion almost blew his chance to repeat. **Sam Mikulak** had a terrible first day, stumbling in several routines. He was several points behind the leaders as the final day of competition began. But Mikulak put the past behind him and performed almost perfectly. He posted great score after great score as the athletes ahead of him each made mistakes. In the end, he was the national champ again. Runner-up **John Orozco** won the vault, one of six different gymnasts to win the six individual event titles.

Biles was super-steady.

Wrestling

No one wore a mask or a weird costume or used a chair to hit anyone in the head. This was collegiate wrestling, not sports entertainment. The nation's top college wrestlers battled at the NCAA Championships.

Penn State and Minnesota looked like the teams to beat. Penn State won two of the weight divisions on the final day, while Minnesota lost its two finals. That gave Penn State its fourth straight national championship. **Ed Ruth** won his third straight title at 184 pounds to help the **Nittany Lions** keep the title in Pennsylvania.

Other key winners included Ohio State's **Logan Streiber** (141 pounds) winning his third straight title, and a pair of freshmen champs, **Jason Tsirtsis** of Northwestern (149 pounds) and **J'Den Cox** of Missouri (197 pounds).

Ruth helped Penn State win it all.

Tour de France
Viva Italia! Welcome Back, France!

Nibali rode him in the champion's famous yellow jersey.

Road cycling is one of the fastest and most exciting outdoor individual sports. But it can also be pretty dangerous. The racers are moving at high speed, just inches from each other. The slightest wobble or slip can turn into a mass, chain-reaction crash. Other than helmets, they wear very little padding.

In the 2014 Tour de France, early wrecks knocked some of the favorites out of the race. British rider **Chris Froome** was hoping to win back-to-back Tours, but after two bad crashes and the resulting injuries, he had to drop out. **Alberto Contador** of Spain has already won twice and was going for three when he crashed and broke his leg midway through the month-long race.

Other than simply surviving, the key to winning the Tour is doing well both in the sprint sections and on the steep mountain climbs. Italy's **Vincenzo Nibali** proved to be the all-around best. He finished second in the mountain stages and sixth in the sprints. As the Tour made its way through Paris for the final stage, he was the easy winner. He was the tenth rider from Italy to win the famous race.

The good news for French fans was that their riders finished second and third. No French rider had finished in the top three since 1997.

Mountain Bike World Cup

If you think the Tour de France riders are brave, check out some mountain-bike racing online. The downhill riders crash through forests, trees, trails, and jumps, while the cross-country riders hit mud, water, rocks, and more. Sometimes they even have to carry their bikes! After the dust, er, mud cleared in 2014, here were the top riders in the World Cup standings.

	MEN	WOMEN
Downhill	Josh Bryceland	Manon Carpenter
Cross-Country	Julien Absalon	Jolanda Neff

Swimming
Familiar Faces in the Pool

That long, lean body splashing through the pool looked pretty familiar. Two years earlier, the world knew exactly who that guy was, as he romped through the London Olympics. But then **Michael Phelps** retired from swimming, so what was he doing back in the pool?

Phelps decided he had more to accomplish, even after winning an all-time record 22 Olympic medals and setting dozens of other records. At 29, however, he would have a hard time keeping up . . . or so some thought.

At the US Nationals in August, he kept up just fine for the most part. Fellow gold medalist **Ryan Lochte** out-touched Phelps in the 200-meter individual medley final. Phelps finished second in the 100-meter butterfly, too. He said he was happy with how he had performed.

Along with Lochte, **Anthony Ervin** was a big winner on the men's side. Though at 33 he was the oldest swimmer in the race, he won the 50-meter freestyle sprint. He had previously won back back in 2001!

On the women's side, **Katie Ledecky** made international headlines with a world record in the 400-meter freestyle. She now owns the world records in the 400-, 800-, and 1500-meter swims at the same time. That's the first time that has happened since **Janet Evans** did it in 2006. But that's no surprise for a swimmer who captured a 2012 Olympic gold and three 2013 world titles.

At the Pan-Pacific Championships later in August, Ledecky kept up her winning ways. She won four gold medals and broke her own world records in the 400 and 1500. Phelps proved that the US meet was a good warmup; he won three gold medals and a silver!

Ledecky added two records to her amazing list of big wins.

AMAZING SPORTS

HANGING EIGHT?
Surfing dogs? Dude, that is radical! Every year, the good folks of Huntington Beach, California, put on the SurfDog contest. Brave doggies of all shapes and sizes (yes, they wear life vests) jump on their boards (with a little help from the humans) and hit the waves. The event raises money for local charities, but it mostly raises smiles and cheers for the four-footed surf doggies. Congrats to Dozer the bulldog, who was named 2013's "Best in Surf." SurfDog's website says that Dozer now has, um . . . "wagging rights" for a year!

He spent a lot of time with US assistant captain **Davis Love III**, but he also got to meet skiing star **Lindsey Vonn**. She was there watching her boyfriend, **Tiger Woods**. In fact, she even put Sammy on Tiger's shoulder . . . without telling him! When the tournament was over, Sammy returned to the woods with some great stories to tell.

▲Sammy the Squirrel

At golf's Presidents Cup (page 160), an uninvited guest got a lot of attention—a very friendly forest dweller nicknamed **Sammy the Squirrel**. Unlike most of his shy cousins, Sammy had no problem climbing up on people.

▼World Cup of Dance?

At the 2014 World Cup (page 66), the Colombian team turned a lot of heads with its offensive firepower. But it also got a lot of attention for something else they did with their feet—dance! After goals, the whole team got together for a mini-samba routine.

World Cup of Books? ▶

Fans of the **Harry Potter** books certainly enjoy reading about Quidditch, the game the Potter characters play. But those readers could become players once someone figured out how to play without actually flying! The 2014 World Cup was held in South Carolina. The team from the University of Texas came out on top in the seventh annual event.

Rocket on the Beach

Beachgoers in Santa Barbara were surprised in July when a giant walked across the sands. Turned out he was there to play kickball! Houston Rockets' star **Dwight Howard** was in town to work out with a trainer. A kickball team heard about it and invited him via Twitter to come out and play. A real kickball league is played every summer on the beach there. Howard pitched for one team, and even took his turn at bat, or should we say, "at foot!"

WEIRD SPORTS WORLD RECORDS

* In March, **Andrew Cowen** of Illinois bowled a game with a score of 280. Pretty good, right? After all, 300 is the most you can get in one game. Oh, yes, did we mention . . . he bowled backward! That's right, he never saw what he was bowling at as he let the ball go. His score set a new world record in a very strange category.

* **Anthony Brooks** set his record while swimming (sort of) so we'll count it. He solved a Rubik's Cube in one minute, 18 seconds. The swimming part? He was underwater the whole time, on one breath!

* Ida Keeling of Ohio set a world record by running 100 meters in 59.80 seconds. Not that fast, right? Well, she was 99 years old at the time!

* Massachusetts resident **Mark Henry** walked down a flight of 77 steps in 30 seconds . . . on his hands! It was not his first upside-down record. In 1995, he held the world record for hand-walking 50 yards.

Sports Kids Rule!

Who says you have to be a grown-up to be a champion? These kids are setting records, turning heads, and putting on a show.

Davis was the talk of the baseball world in 2014.

PHILLY FIREBALLER

The biggest story at the 2014 Little League World Series was a hard-throwing righthander from Philadelphia. **Mo'Ne Davis** became the first girl ever to start and win a game at the World Series. She was on the cover of *Sports Illustrated* after she struck out eight while allowing only two hits in beating Nashville. Though her team lost to Nevada in the next game, she was still the talk of the tournament. Bad news for the Philadelphia Phillies, though, she says her best sport is actually basketball!

DARING DIVER

Jordan Windle has come way up since starting his life as an orphan in far-off Cambodia. He was adopted by American parents and kept going up, all the way to the top of a diving tower. In 2014, he really got to the top. He was just 15 years old when he won the national senior championship in the 10-meter platform event. He had the only 100-point dive of the event on the way to winning by more than 85 points. Needless to say, the next big step up for Jordan will be the 2016 Olympics in Brazil. He'll be a veteran of about 17 then!

FAST-MOVIN' MARY

Keep an eye on **Mary Cain**. At just 16, she's one of America's best distance runners. She holds the American record in the indoor mile race for any age group. She also holds junior records for the 1500-meter, two-mile, and 3,000-meter races. In 2014, she finished second among all racers in the 1500 at the Outdoor National Championships.

FORE...TEEN!

In 2014, golf became a game for young people . . . really young people! A couple of teenagers and one girl who won't be a teen for two years made big news.

- **Lucy Li** became the youngest player ever in the US Women's Open. She was just 11 years old when she teed off in the big event in North Carolina. She didn't finish low enough to make the cut (that means to play the final two rounds), but she gained a lot of fans. As she ate ice cream during a post-match interview, she was all smiles. The reporters asked if she was nervous. "Not really," she said. "I just want to go out there and have fun and play the best I can and I really don't care about the outcome, it's just I want to have fun and learn." Later she added, "I like golf because it's different from other sports. Anybody can play it, if you're tall, short, fast, or slow!"

- The best woman golfer in Canada, pro or amateur, is only 16! **Brooke Henderson** finished tenth at the 2014 US Women's Open. But she's still an amateur, so she couldn't take home the $90,000 she would have won. Brooke has won numerous junior events—she is still in high school, after all! She's headed next to the University of Florida before making the jump to pro golf. Her performance in 2014 shows that she is ready for the big time now!

- Look for more great things from another teen golfer. **Lexi Thompson** was just 19 years, 1 month old when she won the 2014 Kraft Nabisco Championship, one of the women's major titles. She was the second-youngest ever to win a major.

- On the men's side, **Jordan Spieth** is just barely *not* a teenager, but he nearly made it into the record books. At the 2014 Masters, he was in the lead in the third round and finished tied for second overall. Had he won, he would have been the youngest Masters champion ever at the age of 20.

Li's post-round snack? An ice cream cone.

Big Events 2014-15

September 2014

4 Pro Football
NFL regular season began with a matchup between the Packers and the defending-champion Seahawks

7 Basketball
WNBA Finals begin

7–8 Tennis
US Open final matches, New York, New York

8–14 Wrestling
World Championships, Tashkent, Uzbekistan

11–14 Golf
Tour Championship, PGA, Atlanta, Georgia

23–28 Golf
Ryder Cup, Gleneagles, Scotland

30 Baseball
MLB postseason begins (Wild Card playoff games, League Division Series, League Championship Series, World Series)

October 2014

3–13 Gymnastics
World Artistic Championships, Nanning, China

11 Swim/Bike/Run
Ironman Triathlon World Championship, Hawaii

November 2014

2 Running
New York City Marathon

16 Stock Car Racing
Ford Ecoboost 400, final race of NASCAR Chase for the Cup, Homestead, Florida

December 2014

4–13 Rodeo
National Finals Rodeo, Las Vegas, Nevada

5 College Football
Pac-12 Championship Game, California

6 College Football
ACC Championship Game, Charlotte, North Carolina

Big Ten Championship Game, Indianapolis, Indiana

SEC Championship Game, Atlanta, Georgia

6 or 7 Soccer
MLS Cup, Site and specific date TBD

5, 7 College Soccer
Women's College Cup,
Cary, North Carolina

12, 14 College Soccer
Men's College Cup,
Philadelphia, Pennsylvania

31 College Football
Fiesta Bowl, Glendale, Arizona

January 2015

1 College Football

College Football Playoff
Semifinal; Rose Bowl,
Pasadena, California

College Football Playoff
Semifinal; Sugar Bowl,
New Orleans, Louisiana

Outback Bowl, Tampa, Florida

AT&T Cotton Bowl Classic,
Dallas, Texas

Capital One Bowl, Orlando,
Florida

2 College Football
Sugar Bowl, New Orleans,
Louisiana

3 College Football
Orange Bowl, Miami,
Florida

3–4 Pro Football
Wild Card Playoff Weekend

12 College Football
College Football
Championship Game
AT&T Stadium, Dallas,
Texas

10–11 Pro Football
NFL Divisional Playoff
Weekend

17–25 Figure Skating
US Figure Skating
Championships,
Greensboro, North Carolina

18 Pro Football
NFL Conference
Championship Games

22–25 Action Sports
Winter X Games 18,
Aspen, Colorado

25 Football
AFC-NFC Pro Bowl,
Phoenix, Arizona

25 Hockey
NHL All-Star Game,
Columbus, Ohio

25–26 Tennis
Australian Open finals

February 2015

1 Pro Football
Super Bowl XLIX,
Phoenix, Arizona

TBA* Baseball
Caribbean Series,
Puerto Rico

15 Basketball
NBA All-Star Game,
New York City, New York

22 Stock Car Racing
(NASCAR) Daytona 500,
Daytona Beach, Florida

Produced by Shoreline Publishing Group LLC

Santa Barbara, California

www.shorelinepublishing.com

President/Editorial Director: James Buckley, Jr.

Designed by Tom Carling, www.carlingdesign.com

The *Scholastic Year in Sports* text was written by

James Buckley, Jr.

plus **Beth Craig Zachary** (NHL). Fact-checking by Matt Marini.

Thanks to Matt Ringler, Marisa Polansky, Annie McDonnell, Steve Diamond, Deborah Kurosz, Emily Teresa, and the all-stars at Scholastic for all their gold-medal-winning help! Photo research was done by the authors. Thanks to Scholastic Picture Services for their assistance in obtaining the photos.